The
Dan Riley
School for
a Girl

THE
DAN RILEY
SCHOOL FOR
A GIRL

AN ADVENTURE IN
HOME SCHOOLING

Dan Riley

Houghton Mifflin Company

Boston   New York

1994

Library of Congress Cataloging-in-Publication Data

Riley, Dan.
The Dan Riley School for a Girl : a
homeschooling memoir / by Dan Riley.
p. cm.
ISBN 0-395-68719-5
1. Home schooling — United States. 2. Riley, Dan. 3. Teachers —
United States — Biography. I. Title.
LC40.R55 1994
649'.68 — dc20   94-16659   CIP

Printed in the United States of America

AGM 10 9 8 7 6 5 4 3 2 1

ACKNOWLEDGMENTS

The author would like to thank Dr. Marilyn Kennedy for her
wise counsel and valued support during this adventure.

The author gratefully acknowledges the following sources, from which excerpts
were used in both the schooling of Gillian and the writing of this book: *Anne
Frank: The Diary of a Young Girl* by Anne Frank. Copyright 1952 by Otto Frank.
Used by permission of Doubleday, a division of Bantam Doubleday Dell Publishing
Group, Inc. *Childhood and Society* by Erik Erikson. W. W. Norton, 1963. *Demian*
by Hermann Hesse. Copyright 1925 by S. Fischer Verlag. Copyright © 1965 by
Harper & Row. Reprinted by permission of HarperCollins Publishers. *Food in History* by Reay Tannahill. Crown Publishers, 1989. "The Heart of the Matter" by
Mike Campbell, Don Henley, and J. D. Souther. Copyright © 1989 Cass County
Music/Wild Gator Music, ASCAP. *Journey to Ixtlán* by Carlos Castaneda. Simon
& Schuster, 1972. *Love's Body* by Norman O. Brown. Random House, 1966. *The
New Golden Bough* by Sir James Frazer. Criterion Books, 1959. "The Phantom of
the Opera" by Andrew Lloyd Webber, Charles Hart, Richard Stilgoe, and Mike
Batt. Copyright © 1986 The Really Useful Group Ltd. All rights for the United
States and Canada administered by PolyGram International Publishing, Inc. Used
by permission. All rights reserved. "School Days" by Chuck Berry. Copyright ©
1957 Chuck Berry. Isalee Music. *You Can't Go Home Again* by Thomas Wolfe.
New American Library, 1968.

*This book is dedicated to
my first teacher — my mother, Marie.*

CONTENTS

The Dan Riley
School for
a Girl

∽ 1 ∽

ORIENTATION

IN THE SUMMER OF 1991 I was four months into my second tour of duty as the father of an American adolescent, and I was not having a very good time. The causes of my unhappiness, like lost pennies, could be found almost everywhere.

My favorite was society because it's such a big, fat, all-encompassing target and there are already vast armies of scholars, pundits, activists, and talk show hosts fully mobilized against it. Too much sex . . . too much violence . . . too much MTV . . . too much sugar in the diet; too little respect . . . too little discipline . . . too little self-esteem; not enough love . . . not enough God; no more sense of wonder and joy about the world around us. A parent could run any one of them up the flagpole at dawn and by noon there'd be legions of allies gathered on the village green to salute it.

My least favorite cause of my unhappiness was myself. My basic approach to parenting — my basic approach to life — can best be summed up by that old story about the Iowa man who beat a bass drum in front of his house each night before bedtime. When a neighbor asked why he had to bang his drum so loud so often, the man replied, "It keeps the king cobras away."

"Hell, there aren't any king cobras around here for thousands of miles," said the neighbor.

"And as long as I keep beating this damn thing, it'll stay that way," said the man with the drum.

I keep up my own drumbeat by worrying. I worry about lots of things, but most often I worry about the difficulties in raising a teenager in America in the nineties. I worry about teenagers on drugs, in cars, with guns, and under each other in darkened rooms. I worry about teen suicide, soaring dropout rates, and sagging SAT scores. I worry that one night I will go into my teenage daughter's room and find her in bed clutching her pillow and screaming to be saved from a sea of slithering king cobras.

Worry, I sometimes think, is the only way to stop these kinds of things from happening.

The chief beneficiary of all this worry has been my daughter Gillian, although her older sister, Meagan, was not short-changed in this regard. In the first few months after Meagan's birth, I'd guiltily fall asleep while the breastfeeding was in progress, only to be found hours later roaming the bedroom in my sleep, attempting to deliver Meagan from a host of imagined terrors. Roused from her own sleep, so precious to new mothers, Wife Lorna would turn on the light and catch me in numerous illusory heroic acts: I'd be grasping at thin air over a simple door frame, which, in my dream state, was a gnarled tree in a deep forest, with Meagan stranded in the topmost branches; or I'd be crawling amid the dust bunnies under the bed, which for me was a bat-infested cave with Meagan trapped at the center. Once, Lorna awoke, startled, to find me straddling her and pulling on her shoulders, which to my mind was Meagan's little body falling down an icy crevice.

My recurring dream at that time was of Meagan's holding my hand as we walked along the edge of the universe. Then she would let go of my hand, and I would fade off into the void as she smiled sweetly and waved bye-bye. Between Meagan's and Gillian's births, I read *Wonderland* by Joyce Carol Oates. In it, the hero survives a murderous rampage by his father and goes on to become a successful surgeon and father of two. He's a man, it appears, of considerable goodness, intelligence, and sensitivity. But for confoundingly elusive reasons his younger, teenage daughter turns on him. She runs off with a sort of Charlie Manson clone who parades her, nude, around public beaches. She sends postcards and letters home to Dad describing her humiliations in taunting detail.

While I tried to figure out just what Oates was trying to tell me about child-rearing, the gestation period for Gillian was put on indefinite hold. In fact, she may never have happened if Lorna had not been so adamant about her thirtieth birthday. That was her Rubicon. If she passed it as a mother of one, she promised, she would remain a mother of one forever. So I had to resolve some conflicting emotions in a hurry. If I wanted to avoid doubling my chances of meeting the fate of Oates's hero, then I would forgo the opportunity to be a father again. If, on the other hand, we were to be true to the sixties ethos and "replace" ourselves, Lorna and I owed the world another child.

Gillian was born in Burbank, California, on March 17, 1978.

I am often a reminder to myself of a favorite line from "Younger Generation," an old John Sebastian song: "All my deepest worries are my kid's cartoons." But I don't wish to draw too fine a portrait here of myself as Dad the Neurotic. In the summer of 1991, between seventh and eighth grade, Gillian was inspiring some genuine worries that were not mere figments of my imagination. Most disturbing was that she was deep into an academic free fall.

To put it as succinctly as possible, Gillian's seventh-grade experience was a disaster. She failed math; she failed science; she did poor work in English; her highest achievement came in social studies, in which she received a C–. In addition, there was an abundance of negative commentary from her teachers about the way she conducted herself — failing to get to class on time, failing to do homework, failing to pay attention, and, worst of all, failing to take failure seriously.

She had made me one with the fire chief who learns his kid is an arsonist . . . the butcher who has raised a vegetarian. For most of my life I had been consumed by the pursuit of education only to father a daughter who seemed to disdain it.

When I was growing up in Enfield, Connecticut, in the 1950s, we lived across the street from the North School, the elementary school that I attended from kindergarten through fifth grade. It was a boxy, brownstone building with a no-nonsense demeanor, just like the Bigelow Sanford Carpet Mill that industrial giants had planted on the banks of the Connecticut River a few blocks away. Both the school and the mill were surrounded by asphalt and a fence. At the mill, the asphalt was used as a parking lot. At the school, it was used as a playground. Our play equipment amounted to a ball for bouncing and a rope for skipping. Bigelow employed my mother and father, my grandfather, numerous aunts and uncles, and most of our neighbors. The North School educated me and my brothers, our numerous cousins, and all of our friends.

Our family was like most of the families in our neighborhood — indeed, like most of the families in Enfield. My father and mother were high school dropouts, first-generation

Americans, the offspring of Irish and Italian immigrants, respectively. Despite or perhaps because of their own aborted educations, they knew that teachers held the keys to their children's success. It was through them, through their lessons and their good graces, that we would gain entry into the American mainstream.

Their status as teachers entitled them to be treated like divinity. My mother and aunts often beseeched them to lunch, and when our ladies of literacy deigned to accept (they were all ladies then, with names like Sullivan, Boyle, Devine, Lyons — Irish names), the occasion was marked like a holy feast day. Cooking and cleaning preceded the event for days. And when the teachers arrived at the door, they were greeted with a degree of courtesy and respect usually reserved for the parish priest.

Given such glorification, it's little wonder that teaching was to compete with baseball in staking a claim to my future ambitions. As it turned out, I could hit neither a fastball nor a curve, so my choice was effectively narrowed to teaching.

It was not a sorry second choice. I loved teaching. I loved the whole idea of teaching. As a student, I couldn't wait to teach anything new and exciting. I'd set my younger brother Tim up at a makeshift school desk at home, teach him the lesson I'd learned earlier in the day, give him a test, and grade his paper. Just like that, Tim suddenly knew 70 or 80 or 90 percent of something he hadn't known before. It was magic. Someone had enriched my life by passing something of value on to me, and I'd discovered I could double the enrichment by passing it on to someone else.

With such a legacy, why was school going so wrong for Gillian? The answers seemed to lie everywhere, some at my own feet. Through the early seventies, I had thrived on teaching high school in Lebanon, New Hampshire. Among my specialties was a course with the burdensome title of Who Am I?, which attracted hundreds of students. The emphasis was on reading biographical literature and writing autobiographies. After I had passed the initiation process that students impose on teachers and had established some credibility, their life stories began to unfold before me. They were stories filled with the pains and joys of the human condition — stories of beatings, sexual assaults, suicide attempts, drug and alcohol abuse, crime and brushes with crime, recklessness and near death; stories, too, of happy times, proud moments, blissful memories; private aspirations, secret loves, hidden pleasures — all from the pens of teenagers, sometimes written with soaring good humor, always with unflinching honesty, and almost always with dauntless optimism. Those students became for me a golden generation, helping me fulfill my Mr. Chips image of myself as a teacher.

Unlike Mr. Chips', however, mine was not a lifelong commitment to the classroom. In the mid-seventies, when the heady educational experimentation born in the sixties began to give way to the grim back-to-basics movement, I knew it was time to experience life outside the classroom. We decided to explore other possibilities in California, where I learned a very important lesson about the students I had left behind. Having once invited them to open up to me and having set myself up as a point of contact between them and the adult world, they would not be abandoned. The flow of letters was steady. They sent me schedules of Red Sox ball games in the spring; dried, colored leaves in the fall; poems, buds of novels, and news clippings about former students gone bad or good. Ultimately they sent themselves, and at one point three of them were camping out in our small Los Angeles apartment, having arrived by disparate routes but with similar intentions — to reconnect with a teacher who might now help them sort out a bigger bunch of questions — where to live, how to live, with whom to live.

As I tried to forge a new career for myself and tend to my own family, two letters arrived from New Hampshire which would reverberate through the rest of my life. The first read:

Hey Dan,

Remember me? Tall skinny kid, long hair, somewhat of a "Rebel Without a Cause"? Holy Christ, it's been a long time, hasn't it? Dan, an incredible amount of shit has happened to me since my last magical day back in good ol' (never thought I'd hear myself saying that) Lebanon High. I really feel as if I've grown up (God, I hate the sound of those two words!) quite a bit since then. Can't even begin to get all the thoughts and feelings of them down. There's just too much space between head and paper. I'll just give you a brief outline of what is now slightly stale news, but I guess it was the "turning point" of my life as I know it now.

APPROXIMATE DATE 9/7/76

1. Got license back under conditions that if I ever got picked up for ANYTHING within the next two years, automatic loss of license for min. 1 year, max. 4 year period.

2. Month or so before that, fell in love (or thought so at the time) with the first girl I'd gone out with in three (3) years. The little creatures managed to mess my head up so bad, it just wasn't worth the effort to have it done to me again.

A.D. 10/2/76

1. Bought '69 VW for $125. Incredibly good deal. Headed out for week's vacation in Conn. to see T.S.

2. That night we got drunker than drunk, ate two hits of crystal THC, and were snorting horrendous amounts of some evil shit called "locker room" (bought it at local porn shop, a trip in itself) one snort equals 10–30 second BITCHIN' BUZZ. Ran out of beer at about 8:00. All beer buying places close at 7:30 down there, so we got the brilliant idea to come up here (Lebanon) to get beer (A four hour drive that I had just done 3 hrs prior). We hit guardrails along the way, but we just got a bunch of sparks, a good laugh, and a clear road home (roads were packed, but for some reason people seemed to shy away from us). We didn't even stop to check out damages until the next day. It was one of those things that "fit the moment."

We get into Lebanon at 11:45 (a minor miracle) to find the last of the stores closed 5 minutes beforehand. (Talk about pissed. We considered breaking in and stealing two six packs of beer, but for obvious reasons we restrained ourselves.) Got back to Conn. at 5 A.M.

I left for home two days later cuz I missed Ros (girl) so much (*Love Story* or what!?). First thing I did was went up to her house where I find her and her ex-boyfriend, shall I say "together." Left in a very confused and hurt state of being and at a very high rate of speed. Got picked up by pigs for speeding, laid my trip on them. They obviously didn't care or understand the situation at all. Gave me a ticket anyway. (Bye-bye license; bye-bye girl-friend.) Next night got extremely drunk and depressed, and proceeded to total my four-day-old car. Completely. Three of the best things in my life at that time went completely down the tubes in less than 24 hours. It was badder than bad for a couple of days, Dan. But a couple days later I was thinking suicidal thoughts (what I thought was seriously), cuz it seemed like someone (yeah, Him, the Big Guy upstairs) was trying to tell me that this thing called life was just not for me, when I realized that someone (same guy) was trying to tell me something like: "Clean up your act, Asshole, cuz you just got your last warning."

I paid off that VW, decided that Ros wasn't worth fucking up my whole head and life over, went to court, told the judge my story, got found guilty, and appealed it to superior court, which I go to in the springtime. I'm not gonna get picked up for anything until then, at which time I will try to clearly tell the judge what happened, and how incredibly bad things had to get to make me realize how good they could get. I just hope he is still somewhat human and can understand that.

Dan, while I am still basically an insecure person, there is still a nice bright light at the end of the tunnel that keeps me reaching and trying to better myself. All I've got to do is keep on telling myself that I can make it over that rainbow, and that my smallest dreams can come true if I want them to, something I never realized or believed in before. I really think I'm going to make it in this thing called life.

> Thinking of you,
> Bobby

A few months later the second letter arrived:

Dear Dan,
    By now I'm sure someone has told you about Bobby's suicide. If not, forgive me for such an opening line.

I don't know what kind of letter this is going to be, Dan, so bear with me.

Damn it, Dan, I feel like a part of me has died and I'd just as soon let the rest of me go with it. I know the meaning of the word sorrow now more so than I would ever have cared to. It just seems so unbelievable, like something off a TV soap, but these feelings just keep going through my head.

I thought I knew Bobby (famous words) but I guess not enough. We talked a lot about all sorts of things, life, feelings, thoughts, and life again. I knew things were getting him down and he was seeing a lady at Headrest. He really liked her. I was up to his house Sat., 23, and he said then that if he had the money he would have bought some bullets for his gun and killed himself. He was really upset, so I stayed because I was scared for him. He talked. I listened. It was just a few self admissions that he had to get out.

Well anyway I have his journal and would like you to read some of the last parts so you can understand the way I kinda hope I do.

(BOBBY'S JOURNAL)
"Wow, talk about a fucked up nite. I've got to do something about getting my fucking act together. I am paranoid about the most trivial shit!! I can't even carry on a normal conversation with anybody without feeling self conscious about what I'm saying or feeling, and the weirdest part is that for some reason people see me as some sort of leader. But I can't even be sure about that cuz I'm not sure about anything any more. I'm centered on ME and ME only. All the fuckups of my life are just carrying me into a fucking bundle of nerves. I've thought about suicide, but for some reason I keep telling myself that it will all end, that it has to end sometime.

"If I . . . get around somebody . . . just me . . . and then I imagine that I put on a pretty good act or at least I try to, but it feels like I'm being really plastic and fake all the time. I'm not even sure who [I am]!!

"I really feel that I could accomplish a lot of shit at times, but I always fuck myself up. I get even more unsure of myself when I get around a bunch of people. When I get high or drunk . . . and I know what it's going to be like [to] get fucked up, but I keep doing it anyway. I'm all the time worrying about what people are thinking about me. I am a bundle of fucking nerves and I've got to do something about it cuz it is not even a good feeling feeling so sucky all the time. I really don't like the way I am!!! I want to like myself so I can like other people."

(END OF BOBBY'S JOURNAL ENTRY)

It scares the hell out of me, Dan! Drop me a few lines when you can. It would surely be appreciated.

Doug

Teenage lives brim over with so much danger, heartbreak, and confusion. At thirty, I'd either grown too old for their needs or I'd let them get too close to me; either way, their lives had become too hot and unpredictable for me. I wanted a new life; I didn't want to be their father figure or even their teacher anymore. So when the demands of home ownership in New Hampshire forced our return from California and I reluctantly resumed teaching, it was with a totally different outlook than the one with which I had started my career. I would not be consumed by my students again. I was determined to maintain a distance between students and teacher . . . between them — with their uncertainties, anxieties, and desperation — and me.

To this end, I assumed the role of a no-nonsense, strictly-by-the-book teacher. Student evaluation would become a simple matter of mathematics. If one student's grade was 65 and that was passing, that student passed. If another student's average was 64 and that was failing, that student failed. I did not care to know what disadvantages of the heart, the soul, or the mind my students suffered.

It was back-to-basics, thoroughly professional teaching — dispassionate yet competent. And it made me miserable, physically sick, and I took it all home with me to infect the family. Almost daily I railed against the stupidity of a system that made me guard hallways, checking students for bathroom passes; against the timidness of colleagues who allowed doctors and hardware salesmen to bully our profession in ways they'd never allow their own professions to be bullied; and against administrators who ran the school district like dictators. (True quote from the superintendent of schools of Lebanon, New Hampshire, the "Live Free or Die" state: "We tried democracy once in this district, and it didn't work.")

I even railed against the students — their false values, their rudeness, their monumental ignorance. And for good measure Lorna railed against the puny paycheck I was getting for all this grief.

Ours, then, became like countless other American homes where the public schools serve as the private whipping post for myriad personal discontents. Thus the immigrant tradition was broken. Meagan, who was just starting school, and Gillian, who would one day soon, were not to be raised in a home where school was viewed second only to church and teachers seen as almost holy figures, with the wisdom and power to guide us toward a better life.

This alone, of course, was not why Gillian failed seventh grade math and science and did lousy work everywhere else.

Little is that straightforward, least of all where Gillian is concerned.

Gillian is a marvel of human complexity. She is equal parts fascination and exasperation, capable of startling insights and irritating shortsightedness; she can be grandly ambitious about the next twenty years of her life and astonishingly lazy about the next twenty minutes. She takes direction poorly, gives it confidently. She's often little Miss Know-it-all, yet she harbors deep insecurities about her considerable abilities. She aches for the company of others but can torch a relationship in an instant with a flash of temper or an unkind remark.

She can and has inspired uncommon love. A letter from a sixth-grade admirer reads:

Dear Gillian,

I really enjoy talking to you because you are a very funny person and I really think you are so pretty!! I hope we can be SUPER good friends. You are really nice and I wish we could see each other more often because I really love you! If you ever ask me out I would say yes in a millisecond. I would go to the movies with you any day. Although I don't know if you like me as more than a friend, I really hope that this dream will come true. I would do most anything to make you happy. You have the most wonderful looking eyes. They are like stars in the night shining bright. You may think I'm an odd person for watching Conan movies and my unusual interest in archaeology, paleontology, and geology. I really hope you think of me as a good friend. When I am sad you are always there to cheer me up. I bet you think I'm weird for writing a letter this long and so unusual BUT there's a whole lot more. I think of you when I go to bed at night and wake up in the morning. I hope we can be very good friends throughout our life. I was going to put my arm around you when we were at the movies but I was afraid you would go, "Oh, my God!" I don't think I would have enjoyed the movie if you were not there to sit next to me. I really honestly love you. I'm really glad we are such good friends.

        Love you always,
        Andrew

I also consider Gillian the world's greatest practitioner of that bumper sticker advice: QUESTION AUTHORITY. She questions all authority all the time. It is both her strength and her weakness. In her early years her questions had that sort of kids-say-the-darnedest-things charm about them. In learning to read, for instance, she challenged the spelling of why. "Why don't they just spell it y?" she demanded. As she grew older and began to take her questions out of the house, they began to lose a good deal of their charm and frequently fell on adult ears like incendiary devices.

Institutionally, her track record had a certain momentum to it. At age four, in a Montessori school, her teachers gave her high marks for buttoning, snapping, and buckling. They were impressed with her use of scissors, glue, and paintbrush. And they tested and happily found her able to perform simple three-digit addition with sums to 19. In a narrative report one teacher commented, "She is doing a fine job, too, in keeping her talking under control."

We removed her from the Montessori school, however, because she was getting "benched" every day — isolated on a corner bench for a time determined by the infraction. In an effort to support the school, we made a home rule that if she got benched at school she would get benched at home. For two weeks then — or as long as we could stand it as parents — she was getting benched every day, and every night, and in the process found God. Before starting school, she had but a passing acquaintance with a supreme being, since Lorna and I believed individuals should find God on their own. We never expected the process to work so fast, but watching Gillian take to prayer so early and so fervently convinced me that the original discovery of God was probably made under similar circumstances: some Paleolithic problem child begging an imagined, omnipotent force to save her from yet another benching.

In public school, a third-grade teacher filled Gillian's report card with As and Bs but commented that "her constant talking slows her down and disturbs others." By fifth grade, the As had disappeared, and her teacher suggested she needed to show improvement in demonstrating self-control and following rules. By sixth grade, the Bs had practically disappeared, the need for self-control and following rules increased; the teacher lamented that "Gillian is a dynamic personality who needs to focus her enthusiasm on organizational skills and work quality."

Against this background was a series of annual standardized exams that tantalized us with glimpses of the would-be student within — above average in social studies, above average in reading comprehension, the 80th percentile in science, the 90th percentile in math. Even in the wasteland of her seventh grade, she finished way above the national norm in total reading and average everywhere else. This in spite of her admitted effort to get the monkey of being a bright underachiever off her back by randomly picking and choosing her way through the test.

The difficulties at school fueled difficulties at home. The

benchings of her Montessori school days gave way, in public schooling, to constant grounding — or "groundation," as she called it, coining a term that came closer to the ball and chain spirit of her restrictions to home. Her crimes, whether committed at school or at home, were small and actually rather commonplace when viewed against the options she had, growing up in contemporary America. No gangs. No guns. No drugs.

Lots of gum chewing in class, however. Lots of getting to class late. Lots of not getting to class at all, not finishing assigned work on time, not finishing work at all. If she was told to be home at six — and she was always expected to be home at six — she wouldn't get home until six-fifteen or six-thirty. If she was asked to do the dishes by eight, she wouldn't start them until nine. If her phone time was restricted to an hour, she always squeezed in another half hour. If bedtime was ten, she'd be in by eleven. If we were eating grandly, she wanted grilled cheese. To slightly paraphrase the Beatles: we'd say yes; she'd say no. We'd say stop; she'd say go, go, go.

Nothing was easy. She could make every inch of adult prerogative a battleground. And to win the battle one day would mean nothing the next, when she could be back like a relentless little guerrilla army, ready to join the battle all over again. Her capacity for confrontation seemed inexhaustible.

As if the persistent, petty battles over authority weren't bad enough, critical questions of trust began to arise. After a particularly bad report card during seventh grade, she was grounded for an indefinite period of time, starting with a highly anticipated dance at the teen center. The rule of law seemed to be in order that night. Her light was on, with music playing in her room. When I peeked in to check, however, there was nothing but a note that read:

Mom & Dad

I never realized it would hurt so much — hurting someone else. I never cared. It's a shame I had to learn the hard
way — by hurting the two people who brought me into this
world, who watched me grow from 1 foot to 5'4 and who
I care about the most of all. I can't bare [sic] the expressions
on your faces every time you open mail from the school.
I'm sorry. I wish I could relive [sic!] your pain quickly. The
only thing I can do is get out of your hair for a little while,
and sort things out in my messed up brain.
      Love ♥
      Jillian*

PS I ♥ u. Be back soon. I'm safe.

She had aimed for just the right note of mature introspec-
tion and almost reached it. But somehow the apology
sounded just a little too pat, smacked a little too much of the
way troubled teens sum up their problems in the last five
minutes of TV sitcoms. My suspicions went on full alert, and
I headed to the teen center. It didn't take psychic powers to
guess that she had chosen it as the best place for getting out of
our hair. As I led her away from her shocked friends, she tried
to explain that the teen center was merely on the way to her
favorite place for sorting things out in her "messed-up brain."

Shortly after that grounding was lifted, we were awakened
by the parents of her best friend, B, at three in the morning.
The two girls were supposed to be having a sleepover at B's
house that night, but had wandered off at eleven P.M. and
hadn't been seen since. The police were about to call in a

---

*In seventh grade, Gillian started spelling her name with a J. If, when she turns
twenty-one, this turns out to be more than a whim, I'll start spelling it with a J myself,
but here it will be spelled with a G unless, as above, I'm quoting her directly.

helicopter search team when the two girls came ambling up the street. Their story had to do with a nightmare's waking one of them up and then the two of them deciding the best way to get over it was to take a walk through the pitch black of night.

These suburban high jinks are almost laughable, of course, when compared to the horrors faced by parents in South-Central L.A., an hour from our door, where drive-by shootings of children are routine. I should've been thankful for that, but I was too concerned with the direction of Gillian's life for perspective. And my concern was becoming an obsession. It was driving me crazy. I do not exaggerate. I really did go crazy — temporarily, at least. Temporary insanity, in fact, would be my plea for the following behavior.

The exact details leading up to the confrontation are not clear. My memory, which is usually so good about things in general and these things in particular, wobbles pitifully under the burden of carrying this night into the future. I do remember that grandparents were visiting, so my ego involvement was higher than usual. I do remember a lot of shouting going on about who's more important, your family or your friends. I do remember a look of death-defying insolence in Gillian's face.

Suddenly, Gillian and I were alone in the car, heading deep into uncharted territory.

Many years before I had read *Journey to Ixtlán* by Carlos Castaneda, in which his peyote-smoking Indian guide, Don Juan, gave him some advice for a friend who was struggling to raise a difficult child. After the friend had hired an ugly but formidable-looking derelict from skid row, he was to instruct the derelict to follow him and his son to a specified place where, on the cue of some objectionable behavior, the derelict was to leap out, grab the child, and "'spank the living daylights out of him.'"

"'After the man scares him,'" Don Juan said, "'your friend must help the little boy regain his confidence, in any way he can. If he follows this procedure three or four times I assure you that that child will feel differently towards everything. He will change his idea of the world.'"

In raising Gillian I had often been reminded of that passage, and like a child who fantasizes about teaching Mom and Dad a lesson with a suicide attempt, I fantasized about teaching Gillian a lesson with a kidnaping attempt. A few lonely days locked away in some seedy motel on the edge of town, I imagined, would fill her with a proper appreciation for home and family.

Things never got beyond the fantasy stage until that night, when I told her to pick up a sleeping bag and anything she valued and follow me to the car. If she wanted to live without adults interfering with her life, I told her, she was now going to get that chance. We drove off down the longest, wickedest road I could find. She asked where we were going. I told her I was taking her to a spot where she could start a new life free of parental rules. The dark, winding road was finally illuminated by a solitary streetlight. I pulled over to the side of the road and told her: this is it.

She looked out on the desolation, turned to me and said, "Are you trying to kill me?"

I waited for something else . . . my own TV ending where she would throw her arms around me and say, "Oh, Daddy, I've been such a fool! How could I not see that you and Mom really do love me?"

I didn't get it. Instead, she got out of the car and walked away.

One of the most important lessons I had learned as a teacher was, never bluff. Kids will always call you on it, and once they catch you, you've lost your credibility. I never bluffed — until that night. I *was* bluffing, and my own kid was calling me on it. This had been a totally half-assed plan based on the advice of some drugged-out Indian in a book I'd read years earlier. I hadn't even had the good sense to bring along a derelict with me. Operating without a net, I was about to fall.

I started the car again, hoping to inspire a look back. Nothing.

I began to drive away, my eyes glued to the rearview mirror, hoping to catch a glimpse of Gillian, waving tearfully for my return. She just kept walking. I drove a half mile down the road, out of sight, then made a U-turn and came back. She was not to be found. I slammed on my brakes, jumped out of the car, and ran off in search of her. When I found her, I was everything I'd hoped she would be — frightened, chastised, repentant. Even more, I was in awe of her. It was a precocious show of nerves.

I realized on our mostly silent drive home that Gillian was not a kid to be scared or bullied into correct behavior — that this was a child of considerable toughness, and if I ever hoped to reach her, I was going to have to be more rational, more creative, and ultimately more loving than I had been that night.

MATRICULATION

August 15, 1991

Dear Gillian:

On behalf of the faculty and staff of the Dan Riley School for a Girl, I'd like to welcome you for our 1991–92 school year.

You should feel very proud of yourself for being accepted at DRSG since we are very selective in our enrollments. Unlike less discriminating schools that accept students from anywhere else in the world, we don't even accept applications from anyone else. We choose our students, and just like Prince Charles chose Lady Di to be his princess and Richard Gere chose Julia Roberts to be his pretty woman, we chose you to be our one and only student.

We're all looking forward to your arrival for the first day of classes on September 5. Enclosed is our orientation brochure to help you prepare yourself for what promises to be a rich and rewarding experience.

Sincerely,
Dan Riley, Founder and Headmaster . . .
and teacher . . .
and teaching assistant . . .
and head coach . . .

and cafeteria help . . .
and custodial staff . . .
and school crossing guard

The idea for the Dan Riley School for a Girl grew out of the sports pages of the *Los Angeles Times* one morning. I was reading a profile of the Oakland A's manager Tony LaRussa, who is not your typical baseball man. He holds a law degree, campaigns for animal rights, and once a year dons ballet slippers and dances in the *Nutcracker Suite*. What really got my attention, though, was the news that Tony's wife, Elaine, had educated both of their children at home.

It was not the first I'd heard about home schooling, of course. In my own public school days, we were all driven toward an appreciation of the three Rs by stories of Abe Lincoln's struggles to educate himself by candlelight. Our history, in fact, abounds with examples of notables — Thomas Jefferson and Thomas Edison, for instance — who never answered a roll call, never marched in single file to assembly, and never worked on a senior prom committee. Home schooling would seem at first glance, then, to provide a rich training ground for presidents and geniuses.

Or eccentrics. I once knew a couple — cut from the classic California cultist mold — who were devotees of a guru who taught that the answer to all our social problems was insurance; they planned on taking their son out of school and teaching him at home according to the world's great actuarial tables. I also once met an old Vermont hippie who was already educating his children at home. Our brief meeting was long enough for me to recognize that his children would be well versed in composting, astrology, and the music of the Grateful Dead.

I'd certainly never considered home schooling an option for the Riley family. We were too mainstream for that. Jefferson and Lincoln notwithstanding, home schooling struck me as both too far left and too far right — too much for the religious fundamentalists, the nuclear survivalists, and the unregenerate counter culturalists. My kids, I believed, would be educated the way their mom and dad had been — the good, old-fashioned American public school way. And I held firmly to that belief until Gillian put the finishing touches on her first year in junior high school.

I could have rationalized Gillian's difficulties away as generic to her age. As a stage of life, I think puberty is a Frankenstein creation if ever there was one. Libidos of sixteen-year-olds grafted onto ids of five-year-olds. Moral, emotional, and intellectual anarchy reigning supreme. And junior high, under the best of circumstances, has always struck me as being a bit like the bar scene in *Star Wars*, filled with a wide assortment of grotesqueries from alien worlds: girls with elephantine noses — or noses they think are elephantine, and insecurities that certainly are, and boys with prices on their heads — or who act as if they have prices on their heads, and certainly have chips on their shoulders — all wildly intoxicated on their own hormones and spoiling for a fight or a love affair that will transcend the ages.

We could also blame her problems on the schools — an almost irresistible scapegoat. Statistical evidence of their failure is abundant. In 1991 American students placed eleventh worldwide in math competency, which gave rise to great national hand-wringing and further anxiety about the quality of our schools. (However, I've never heard anyone explain what a ten-point differential between first and eleventh place on an international math test means in sheer practical terms.)

Most adults I know have an unsettling anecdote or two about an encounter with a public school student who displays a tenuous grasp on what we once regarded as the basics of a sound education. My own such story unfolded mere days before starting the home schooling. I went to my local video shop to rent *Pal Joey*. As the teen at the counter was checking me out, he asked how I managed to find that particular title. I told him that I went to the music section because it's a musical and I looked under the Ps because *Pal Joey* begins with a *P*.

He said, rather astonished, "The alphabet helped you?"

When I assured him it did, he said he was happy to hear that because, he explained, he had just been made to arrange all the videos in alphabetical order, and he thought it was a waste of time. "I didn't think anybody ever used the alphabet to find a video," he told me. He didn't say how he thought people found videos, but I was glad to be able to verify the value of the alphabet for him — and glad, too, that his teachers had taught him enough so that he could get *Pal Joey* between *Oklahoma!* and *Pennies from Heaven*.

There's a great deal of nostalgia about the good old days of American public education. They seem good to me too, although not particularly rigorous academically. My most vivid recollection of my elementary school teachers is that they excelled at teaching manners and conventions above all else. I can remember bringing my brother's milk money down to Miss Sullivan's first-grade class and wearing my collar up in honor of James Dean, who had just died. There was a great deal of concern about juvenile delinquency back then, and of course the surest sign of a boy gone bad was a turned-up collar. So Miss Sullivan did her bit to save me from going the full JD route — sideburns, black leather jacket, a sneer, and long, idle hours on the street corner. She took me aside and turned my collar down and said, "There. You're not that kind of a boy."

What significantly set that incident apart from today's school environment, I think, is that Miss Sullivan was not taking a risk in touching a student's clothes and venturing a judgment on what kind of boy he was. She didn't have to worry about unleashing a tirade from the student or his parents about his rights. This is not to suggest that student rights is not a legitimate issue. As both a student and teacher myself, I have witnessed numerous infractions of those rights, and it's well that they be treated with respect — which is not to be confused with reverence. But sometimes I think that we'd all be a lot happier and a lot better off today if teachers — and parents — could express themselves clearly and freely about what kind of boys — and girls — we are or ought to become.

Without giving Miss Sullivan any back talk or attitude, just my brother's milk money, I left her room, walked up to the second floor, exercised my right to pull my collar back up, and returned to my classroom. I thought I had the last laugh, but here I am, forty years later, and Miss Sullivan's words are still with me.

Nevertheless, I have resisted the temptation to pin my unhappiness with Gillian's progress as a student and citizen on the public school system. Out of loyalty to and sympathy for my former profession, I would spare that poor dead horse a further beating. Furthermore, the schools in Thousand Oaks, California (where we settled after leaving New Hampshire for good in 1980), are better than average; they are the kind of schools people seek rather than try to escape. Finally, I've never believed that the American educational system is the cause of the decline and fall of the country, as many have alleged. Our school system is nothing but a reflection of society at large. We may do all the finger wagging we want at substandard schools, mediocre teachers, dumbed-down tests, and doped-up students; it only serves to save us from pointing the finger at ourselves and the largely narcissistic, aimless, fragmenting society we've let develop that doesn't seem to know what its legacy, goals, or ideals are any longer — let alone how to maintain an educational system capable of passing any of it along to future generations.

On January 3, 1992, the *Los Angeles Times* reported on the front page that a congressionally appointed advisory panel had concluded that it was time for the United States to adopt a set of national curriculum standards for our schools. This, of course, is not a new idea. I even did a research paper on the subject when I was in high school, about thirty years ago. The big news this time around, according to the article, was that this recommendation "represents a rare consensus among administration officials, education-minded governors, congressional leaders, teachers' unions and other education groups. And they suggest that in its drive to improve the schools, American education may be moving away from the decentralization of policy and curriculum that has always been its trademark."

One panel member optimistically predicted that the national standards ought to be ready for full implementation in five to ten years. Judging by the recent past, we can pretty well guess how painful and protracted it will be to devise these standards. Can any disparate group of Americans agree on anything anymore? A suggestion, for instance, that every math student know that there are twelve inches in a foot and three feet in a yard will surely be challenged by those who maintain that we need to get serious about the metric system — which will be counterattacked by some group claiming that there's something distinctly American about inches, feet, and yards and that the metric system is the tool of insidious globalists bent on robbing us of our national identity. A suggestion that the biological functions of plant and animal structures be taught to all our science students will surely offend religious fundamentalists, who will insist that the divine hand be included in any discussion of the rutting habits of rats. And after the wild controversy over the Columbus quincentenary celebration in 1992, there should be no doubt that it will be difficult to agree on a basic history curriculum that might suggest that Columbus discovered America in 1492. Was it a discovery or a conquest, an unveiling or a rape, the birth of a New World or the death of Eden?

Around our house in the summer of 1991, however, the issue was not the future of America's public schools but Gillian's future. It was becoming alarmingly clear to both Lorna and me that her chances of emerging from public school with anything more than a reputation for goofing off and underachieving were dwindling fast. Gillian herself tried to assure us that she was just going through a stage, and maybe she was. But lemmings go through stages too, I countered, and the last one's a killer. As a parent, I wasn't willing to sit around waiting to see how things developed. I had the profound sense that the time for action had arrived, and if I didn't seize the moment, all the years of worrying what might happen to her life would soon be replaced by regrets over what did happen.

So when I read about Elaine LaRussa's educating her two girls at home in the sports pages of the *L.A. Times* that morning, it was pure serendipity. Of course, I said to myself, I'll educate Gillian at home! All I needed to do was quit my job, negotiate terms with the state of California, and talk Gillian into spending five hours a day in close quarters with her father rather than her friends.

It was not an idea without its problems.

The first person I had to convince was Lorna. In the past, the mere suggestion of a private school education for Gillian had elicited strenuous objections. Having graduated from and taught in public schools herself, Lorna defended them fiercely as democratizing institutions. Although I knew she shared my concerns about Gillian, I also knew she would not stand by loyally to rubber stamp my idea of a home school. She would ask me questions — tough ones. So I decided to get as many answers as I could before I even broached the subject with her.

Fortunately, keeping my job while I taught Gillian at home would not be my hardest problem. My employer allowed me to work at my job in corporate publications part-time from September to June. It was also willing to design a forty-hour work week for me so I could maintain my full-time salary. But the demands on my time and energy would have been severe and would have effectively removed me from any meaningful interaction with the rest of my family. By working part-time, of course, and taking a 50 percent cut in pay, I would be assuring Gillian of a very expensive education. But whatever the cost, I was willing to pay it, because I was convinced by that time that Gillian needed a radical change in the direction of her life.

Dealing with the State of California was not as clear cut. Although the LaRussas (hardly one of California's lower-profile families) had taught their children at home, I couldn't help but wonder if there might be something slightly illegal about it. I had unsettling visions of trying to teach Gillian about meiosis and mitosis one morning while squads of truant officers surrounded the house.

I approached the problem as delicately as possible, calling a range of education bureaucracies from the local to the state level anonymously. Basically, I wanted to know what I would owe the educational establishment if I wanted to teach my own daughter at home. I received a couple of surprising responses. The first was that no one I talked to was openly hostile to the idea, although I was essentially telling these people that I was planning on taking my business elsewhere. One person asked me, reasonably enough, to make sure I was doing the right thing for Gillian since it was such a radical move. Another said she'd heard about a number of people in the state who were already doing what I was planning to do. And a third told me she'd do the same thing if she were in my shoes. I was also surprised that there was very little anyone could tell me about such a process. Each call directed me to another source, and each subsequent call led me to conclude that I should leave well enough alone and just go ahead and do it.

When I finally came upon the book *Homeschooling for Excellence* by David and Micki Colfax, I found that their recommendation was to do just that. Let sleeping dogs lie, in fact, could pretty much serve as the motto for the home schooling movement as it concerns the educational establishment. Nevertheless, I felt there was too much at stake to take a chance on being shut down or becoming embroiled in a legal dispute, so I pushed on in my search for state sanction. I finally received a document from the legal department of the state board of education that outlined three acceptable ways of teaching a child at home. The first was that a teacher with state credentials tutor the child. The second was that the home school constitute itself as a private school. The third was that the parent coordinate a program through the student's public school. I preferred the third alternative, seeing it as a way of making sure Gillian was on course with her peers and as a curriculum and materials resource for me. Unfortunately, I learned, our school district had no such program for junior high students.

That left the other two alternatives, which both had minor drawbacks. With a teaching credential from New Hampshire, I had only to pass an exam, fill out some forms, and pay some fees to receive a credential in California. That sounded pretty easy, but despite having two degrees to my name, I really wondered: What if I flunk? What if I can't cut it any longer — testwise? What if the State of California asked me to find the value of x and I was exposed as one more dunderheaded American suffering from innumeracy? The problem would be twofold — with the state and with my ego. And ego was no small factor in this venture: essentially I was saying to the world that I could do what an army of professionals had failed to do in nearly eight years — turn Gillian Riley into a happy, productive student.

I decided to hedge my bet and pursue both alternatives. Simultaneously with brushing up on my algebra, I secured the documentation necessary to define our home as a school. The only problem was that the state seemed purposely vague in this area. The main document it sent me was entitled Private School Affidavit. It asked for some very rudimentary information — name of school, number of students enrolled, administrator, and so on. It also asked for a fire and health inspection. The state, however, clearly labeled this document an affidavit, not a license, to operate a private school; its exact words were: "The Department of Education does not license, evaluate, recognize, approve, or endorse any private school or course." Given the idiosyncratic nature of certain private and/or home schools, it struck me as a sensible state policy. The majority of home schools, to be sure, have been established on ideological or religious grounds, and it would really compromise the state, I guess, if it started handing out its imprimatur to little academies run by political or theological extremists. On the other hand, if the state ever got wind of hooded children taking field trips to minority-owned businesses or animal sacrifices in church basements, it had to have room to maneuver. That, I concluded, was why it gave itself a back-up position later in the affidavit. Under the heading Licensing, the state says, "In addition to filing the affidavit, the owner of the school should contact the appropriate municipal or county authorities to ascertain the applicable ordinances involving business licensing, safety, law enforcement and property use regulation . . ." Enough red tape was buried in that clause to trip up the most meticulous educator.

In my eagerness to comply, I called zoning departments, offices of building safety, and the like, and was told by each that no one knew anything about inspecting, certifying, authorizing, or categorizing a home as a private school. I was beginning to get the message. No one was really going to stop me from establishing a school in our home, but no one was going to issue me a document with the state seal of approval on it, either. I was going to have to be satisfied with my measly affidavit, which, inconsequential as it may have been, at least served as an official announcement to the world that the Dan Riley School for a Girl existed.

Announcing it to the world was one thing, announcing it to the family was quite another.

My original plan was, quietly and methodically, to enlist Lorna's support before ever mentioning it to Gillian, but one summer night it just broke into the open when she asked about shopping for school clothes. I couldn't resist saying something like, "You may not have to worry about school clothes this year." Gillian quickly countered, "What do you mean by that?" And her uncle Tim, a lawyer, who happened to be over for dinner that night, suddenly did this Perry Mason thing and announced my guilt before anyone even suspected me of a crime. "You won't need school clothes because your father's going to teach you at home," he said.

It was a shot in the dark, pure and simple. Too many years of being a brother, I guess, or maybe I'd been giving off intimations of my plan that I hadn't realized. In any case, everyone knew there was something to it immediately because I cannot count a poker face among my natural gifts. A certain levitation process then went to work in the room as I laid out my plan. Even Gillian, who, like most teenagers, is a master at feigning indifference to any subject that seems to animate adults, moved out of her noncommittal slouch onto the arm of her chair and leaned forward. "You mean we can do that?" she asked incredulously.

I liked that reaction. I had never expected her to throw her arms around me and say, "Oh, Daddy, what a neat idea!" But I was confident that as long as she didn't do this *Exorcist* thing with the spewing pea soup and the head spinning, we'd have something we could build on. "You mean we can do that?" was not bad. There was a little surprise, a tiny sense of adventure, and just a hint of expectation. I could build on that. I was sure I could build on that. But first I was going to have to answer a few objections.

Lorna raised the first: my perceived inadequacies in math

and science. Although I worked for a company engaged in scientific research and dealt with math on a regular basis, I was clearly from the humanities tribe. I had struggled with math as a student myself and had expressed little interest in science. As a father, I cultivated an image of incompetence in both areas if for no other reason than to save myself from having to help out with math homework and the dreaded annual science fair projects. But secretly I had changed. I no longer felt oppressed by math, as I had when, as a teenager, it threatened to ruin my entire life, or at least the weekend preceding any and all math tests. And, my respect for science, like broccoli, had grown as I matured and came to appreciate scientific inquiry as the only path to true knowledge. Besides, I argued — with both myself and others — I'm going to be teaching an eighth-grader, not a grad student at Caltech. Certainly I could master these subjects enough to teach Gillian a little something about dividing with decimals or random selection. It was not, admittedly, the most convincing case, but since it wasn't the strongest of the three objections, it didn't have to be.

It would take a lot more to persuade the doubters that Gillian and I would not be at each other's throats within a week. I remember another bumper sticker from my teaching days: PARENTS ARE TEACHERS TOO. But no one seems to believe it — least of all parents and their kids. It's as if once we've taught them how to talk, walk, and use the toilet, we have nothing more than money to offer. Lorna was most vocal on this subject since she, who once taught Chopin to the children of total strangers, had already tried to teach piano to Gillian. Her recollections of that hellish experience are vivid and disturbing. (We have a theory, in fact, that all heavy metal groups consist of boys who were once taught an instrument at home by their parents. Their music is now their vengeance on the world.)

To add to the pessimistic projections was the unhappy fact that the recent relations between Gillian and myself could best be described as antagonistic. While Lorna virtually brimmed over with the mother's milk of kindness and understanding, I fell into the traditional paternal role of disciplinarian. Gillian and I were Jean Valjean and Inspector Javert: I could be unrelenting in pursuit of justice no matter how small or natural the crime. We were Professor Moriarty and Sherlock Holmes: my mental acuity could turn partially overheard phone conversations or pieces of shredded notes into clues to dark, diabolical conspiracies. We were Luke Skywalker and Darth Vader, child and parent, each trapped on opposite sides of the Force.

Gillian and I had already locked horns a few times on the battlefield of learning, most memorably when I took on the task of toilet training her. As Lorna was working full-time and I was a teacher with plenty of time off and lots of dirty diapers to fill it, I had plenty of incentive for throwing myself into the duty. I even suspended my disbelief and accepted a book from a friend, *How to Toilet Train Your Child in a Day.* Briefly, the book tells the parent to bring the child and a favorite doll together, offer them both unlimited refills of a fruit drink until the baby's bladder is full, then march them both to the toilet. The parent then props the doll on the toilet, provides appropriate sound effects, and praises the doll, rewarding it with M&Ms. The baby is then offered a chance to earn some M&Ms with a similar performance. It sounded absolutely foolish, certainly not like something that would work in a day. But with few strategies of my own, I tried it.

Within an hour, Gillian was taking her pee on the toilet. By naptime, she had brilliantly analyzed this process as a means of manipulation. I'd put her down, and within minutes she was calling me back to take her to the toilet — again and again and again. She was holding out the promise of the big payoff, the grand slam of toilet training. And I wanted it too — the prize to show off to wife and mother, big sister and grandparents. But it never came, and it became clear by the fifth try that Gillian was playing me like a yo-yo. So on that fifth trip to the toilet I propped her up on it and sat down on the edge of the tub, determined to wait her out until I heard that coveted plop in the water. Soon, however, her little legs gave out and she went plop herself. I fished her out, dried her off, and put her back for her nap for good. In another two days we hit pay dirt, but the dynamics of our working together had pretty much been framed for the future.

To alleviate the possibility of a bloodbath over a morning geography lesson, I promised to become Jekyll and Hyde — an open, understanding, kindly bearer of the world's wisdom by day, a rule-giving, curfew-enforcing, father-fiend of the night. Neither Lorna nor Meagan believed it could really be done — not without chemicals, at least — but interest in seeing me try was growing. The homework I had done convinced them I was serious and everyone, including Gillian, realized that she couldn't continue on her present course.

The final objection, which seemed to me at the time to be the least worrisome, concerned Gillian's social life if she were not attending public school. In fact, that has been the first and most frequently asked question of friends, relatives, and mere acquaintances when the talk turns to home schooling. That's probably a good indicator of the status schools hold as agencies of socialization, not to mention the premium placed on the socializing process itself. It's truly a who-you-know, not what-you-know, world out there, and not for just the advantages of who you know but for the comfort it brings as well.

Much to my later regret, I blithely dismissed this particular concern; if Gillian had succeeded at anything in school, it had been at building up a strong, vast network of friends who tied up our phone for hours, wrote volumes of notes to one another, and stalked the shopping mall in packs as tight and eternal as wolves. I assured Gillian she'd have more time with her friends than ever because, given the schedule I was devising, her school obligations would be done at 3 P.M. — all done. She'd be able to meet with her friends right after school or talk on the phone at length without having me or homework hovering over her.

I believed it, and Gillian bought it.

Well, *bought* may be overstating the case. I think that in a totally free universe, Gillian wouldn't have bought any of this. She would have returned to public school, promised to do better, and let come what may. But I think the utter extraordinariness of my plan impressed upon her how seriously we viewed her academic condition, and she seemed inclined, for both her parents' and her own sake, to give it a chance.

⤺ 3 ⤻

THE FIRST DAY

Up in the morning and off to school
The teacher is teaching the Golden Rule,
American history and practical math
You're studying hard and hopin' to pass
Workin' your fingers right down to the bone
The guy behind you won't leave you alone.

— Chuck Berry, "School Days"

THE FIRST DAY of our home school was scheduled for a Thursday, the same day as the beginning of public school. At 6 A.M., an hour and a half before the "first bell," I was doing a series of 180-degree turns in my bed, thinking about what I was going to say and do when I met my student under classroom conditions for the first time. With my head buried beneath a couple of pillows and a blanket, I came up with the idea to start the day off with a musical selection — something classical, I thought . . . something from the Chuck Berry opus, perhaps. I leapt from my bed and bounded down the hallway toward my record collection. I would find "School Days" there on *Chuck Berry's Greatest Hits*. Berry's description of a typically frenzied American school day would nicely counterpoint the *lycée*-like atmosphere of the Dan Riley School for a Girl and subtly remind our student of how lucky she was.

> Ring, ring goes the bell
> The cook in the lunchroom is ready to sell
> You're lucky if you can find a seat
> You're fortunate if you have time to eat
> Back in the classroom open a book
> Even the teacher don't know how mean she looks

I couldn't find my Chuck Berry record. Digging around on my knees, deep in the dust below the CDs, the audio cassettes, the 33 rpms — no Chuck Berry. I checked and double-checked. Still no Chuck. Class would be starting soon, and I still had to get washed, shaved, and dressed. What could I use? Jimi Hendrix doing "The Star-Spangled Banner" at morning assembly?

I grabbed *The Phantom of the Opera*, recently seen by the entire family and fresh on the lips of one and all. It was pure happenstance; the irony of the choice wouldn't occur to me until later.

> In sleep he sang to me,
> In dreams he came
> That voice which calls to me
> And speaks my name
> And do I dream again?
> For now I find
> The Phantom of the Opera is there
> Inside my mind

When my eyes first met Gillian's there in our kitchen for the opening moment of our home schooling adventure, familiarity suddenly and mysteriously metamorphosed into strangeness. Years of being her father, of living under the same roof together, no longer mattered. It was like every first day of school I'd ever known as both student and teacher — tentative, full of nervous anticipation and inexplicable shyness — just like a first date. And none of my teaching experience nor my role as father did anything to rescue me from the suffocating need I suddenly felt to do the one thing males have always felt obliged to do in front of females — impress.

I was prepared, however. On the counter was a loaf of risen bread dough about the size of the *Hindenburg*. I had put it out the night before so we could begin the day with a cooking lesson. We would make zeppoli — fried bread dough covered with powdered sugar and cinnamon — a favorite of Gillian's; because of the versatile curriculum of our school, she would henceforth be able to make it for herself at will. She registered neither surprise nor delight, but cast that teenage look of studied indifference at the task at hand.

While she accepted her first assignment and began pounding the bread down before cutting it up into bite-size pieces, I was responding to another inspiration. Of course! We should extrapolate our cooking lesson into other areas — science, maybe, literature, mathematics. I would do exactly what should be done in the public schools but can never be done because the system discourages improvisation. I plucked Reay Tannahill's fascinating *Food in History* from the cookbook shelf, looked up *yeast* in the index, and began to read aloud:

"It was reputedly in Egypt that the art of making modern bread was discovered, although the evidence is elusive and the date even more so. Conditions, however, were favourable, because wheat was the important factor and specifically wheat that did not have to be parched before threshing." I paused and thought, Does Gillian know what *parched* means? Does she know what *threshing* means?

Her back had been to me during my reading, so I had no

way of knowing whether the look on her face had evolved from indifferent to quizzical. I decided to read on:

"The starchy endosperm . . ."

Gosh, endosperm. Surely they taught her *endosperm* at school. If that's not a school word, what is, I thought before continuing:

"The starchy endosperm of wheat contains gluten-forming proteins. Yeast, the other essential ingredient of raised bread, in favourable conditions produces carbon dioxide gas. If the two ingredients are brought together in a bread mix, the result is a spongy mass consisting of tiny gas bubbles each enclosed in an elastic skin of gluten."

"*Voilà!*" I declared, pointing to the bread board where the mighty *Hindenburg* had moored itself. Now it had been thoroughly ripped asunder, reduced to several dozen ersatz doughnut holes.

"Now what?" Gillian asked, uninspired.

As I instructed her on the art of heating oil, Lorna passed by on her way to work. "How's it going?" she asked.

"We're learning all about yeast," I exclaimed. "Listen to this." And I picked up Tannahill and began to read further:

"Coarse flour, even when leavened, still makes a heavy, close-textured loaf, and the worn teeth of surviving skulls show that most Egyptians went on chewing their way through bread made from the old flours, rough with bran and spiky with splinters of chaff (sometimes with splinters of grinding stone as well)."

"Amazing," said Lorna, clearly more in a hurry than amazed. As she waltzed out the door to the accompaniment of our morning soundtrack, she asked if, in the absence of a basement, I would be taking my protégée off to the attic for lessons.

Sing once again with me
our strange duet
My power over you
grows stronger yet
And though you turn from me
to glance behind
The Phantom of the Opera is there
inside your mind

The oil was hot. Time to throw the doughnuts in. I picked up Tannahill and turned to the index under *frying*. Nothing there. Good thing, too. Who knows where it all might have ended? Or if it would have ended. Readings from a chapter on stoves, maybe? Eating utensils? The role of cinnamon in the spread of the Roman Empire?

Gillian turned to me for the first time and said, "I don't know who's going to eat all these things."

"We are," I proclaimed. "You and I."

"Not me," she said. "I'm having Slim Fast for breakfast."

Not me? Not I? I couldn't even deal with her grammar. The smell of mortar was in the air, a wall going up between us. It was a normal time to be hurt or angry. But a voice inside me kept saying, This is a test. This is only a test — a snap quiz at worst. So I held the anger and the hurt in check and calmly said, "I can't believe you're going to pass up your very own first batch of these for Slim Fast." And I left it at that.

We then went over our schedule for the weeks ahead. I explained that one of our projects would be to set up a mock life for her on the computer: getting her a job she might like one day, a car, a home. Then we'd set up a budget, and she'd keep track of her expenses — mortgage, car payments, taxes.

"No taxes," she said in her first show of emotion of the day. "I'm not paying any taxes."

No taxes? I said to myself. Who are the spiritual icons of this generation? Howard Jarvis? Leona Helmsley? I looked at the calendar: 1991. My daughter had grown up during the George Bush years, when cheap demagoguery about "no new taxes" had replaced the tough questions about who pays, how much, what it's for, and what can we do to make sure it's spent wisely. Some presidents inspire the young to join the Peace Corps. Some inspire them not to pay taxes.

I made a quick note for myself to come up with a unit on taxes, observing that Gillian had dipped her hand into the bowl of zeppoli and was popping one into her mouth. By the time we were discussing the rest of our schedule, she'd knocked off about a dozen, washing them down with a glass of Slim Fast.

In my younger teaching days, I would have involved Gillian in the creation of our curriculum almost from the start. Then, my two main influences were A. S. Neill's classic *Summerhill* and Neil Postman and Charles Weingartner's provocative 1972 book, *Teaching as a Subversive Activity.* If our home schooling had been merely an opportunity to indulge my youthful romance with Summerhill, I would have simply filled our classroom, our home, with the tools of learning — books, pictures, videos, maps, computers, a garden, an aquarium, and the like, and every day Gillian would wake up and pursue whatever interested her most while I stood by as an able and caring resource and facilitator.

I could have furthered the fantasy with a nod to Postman and Weingartner. They argued that children have a natural sense of inquiry that schools tend to blunt by trying to turn them into regurgitators of information rather than seekers; a curriculum that followed students' questions to their logical conclusions would probably make for a livelier — and ultimately more logical — learning environment than one based on packaged knowledge. I had never been able to experiment with more than pale imitations of either approach in public school. At home, however, I was free of the dictates of boards of education and the obligation not to use other people's children as guinea pigs. This was my school, my child, so I could be as radical as I wished. However, the teaching at the Dan Riley School for a Girl would be neither Summerhillian nor subversive. The idea of the home school was experimentation enough for one year, I concluded. I would be open to any thoughts Gillian might have on our direction and I would eagerly accept her questions, but our basic curriculum would be fairly orthodox and largely teacher-driven. As much as I may have desired an entirely student-generated curriculum, I had no idea how long our school would last. So I felt compelled to keep the curriculum strictly in line with what I determined were my three main goals.

In *Journey to Ixtlán,* Don Juan speaks of the need to "stop the world" every once in a while. That was clearly one of my goals. I wanted to momentarily stop the world for Gillian — stop her downward spiral, stop the avalanche of bad notices, and give her a time-out, a chance to reflect on where she was taking her young life.

I also wanted her to come out of the experience with a better attitude toward learning. Her seventh-grade performance — constantly getting to class late or not at all or faking her way through homework to sneak in another late phone call — had made it clear that she viewed schoolwork as a major and unnecessary intrusion on her social life.

Most important, I wanted a better relationship with her. I was tired of being Dr. No, always telling her what she couldn't do. I was also weary of my own anxieties, and didn't relish being a slave to them through the next four challenging years of her life. I wanted to know her better because only then, I believed, could I trust her to act responsibly when she was on her own.

Measuring the success of these goals seemed problematical. Stopping the world for her was easy enough: we did that just by pulling her out of public school. Whether she would use the time to reflect on and reassess her life could not possibly be tested objectively.

With a new attitude toward learning, in my wildest dreams — the good wild dreams, the ones without snakes and bats and so forth — she might emulate the sons of David and Micki Colfax, who went straight to Harvard after years of home schooling; she might return to public school and become an A and B student again; or she might just earn a bumper sticker for my car: MY CHILD IS AN HONOR STUDENT AT THE DAN RILEY SCHOOL FOR A GIRL. In nine months, however, we were not likely to have enough tangible evidence of academic growth with which to dazzle the world.

My most important goal, a better relationship, would be the hardest to measure. Without benefit of a parallel universe, we could never know if our relationship were better or worse. A father-daughter relationship is a lifelong thing, and like most such relationships it's subject to peaks and valleys. Maybe we had hit an inevitable low point in that seventh-grade year and were, unbeknownst to ourselves, poised for a natural rebound? Maybe the home school would fail to such a degree that it would damage our relationship forever? Speculating on the road not taken is one of the most tormenting games people play, and with the home school in place, I had given myself all the pieces necessary for playing the deluxe version of the game for a very long time.

I avoided asking Gillian about her goals for the year because I was afraid of her answer. I thought she'd say something like: I just want to get through it. She may have fooled me — and gratified me — by saying, I want to learn as much as I possibly can. But I didn't chance it. Fair or not, I didn't want to leave any openings for negativity about the home schooling, surely not in the early going.

That guardedness did not extend to the outside world. Incorporating the morning newspaper into the curriculum might strike a number of home schooling parents as being downright perverse: for many of them, the rationale for home schooling is to shut out the world. They might argue that newspapers — all media — are the main purveyors of the sex, violence, and overall godlessness that surrounds us. But I thought that this just raised an important question for Gillian and me to consider. If we live in a culture with an excess of sex and violence on its mind and a dispiriting emptiness at its soul, is it because the media make it so or merely reflect it? Rather than answer that question arbitrarily for Gillian — which I couldn't if I'd wanted to — I wanted to teach her to read the paper, to understand the development of stories, to be alert to biases in reporting, to appreciate differences of opinion, and to deal honestly with events and information that may not conform to her own cherished view of the world.

Our primary source in this study would be the *Los Angeles Times*, which, like any good newspaper, can be a valuable learning tool. There's a diversity of opinion on its op-ed pages. In its editorial positions, reason generally prevails over ideology. Page 1 offers Column One, a magazine-length feature that takes a more reflective look at a story that may have dominated the news in previous weeks or expands on a story that may have escaped notice the first time around. Numerous column inches are occasionally contributed by an ombudsman, who can take the paper to task for mishandling earlier stories. And a conscious effort is made to expand our view of the world and what's newsworthy; on Mondays an entire page was given over to science, for instance, and on Tuesdays there's an entire section of reports from around the world.

This is not an advertisement for the *L.A. Times*. In the process of designing a curriculum for my own child, I clarified some of my own values, and some subsidiary goals of a home school began to emerge. I hoped that in the end Gillian would value diversity of opinion, reason over ideology, reflection and substance, self-criticism, and an ever widening view of the world.

"So what do you think of this front page?" I asked her out in the gazebo, where we had reconvened class that first morning.

She soberly looked at that day's paper, spread out before us on a picnic table, and said, "Very boring."

It was September 5, 1991. The Soviet Union was falling apart. A few of the headlines were:

POWER REALIGNMENT BLOCKED
BY DEFIANT SOVIET LAWMAKERS

GORBACHEV POISED TO
RECOGNIZE THE BALTICS

GLOBAL STRATEGY ELUDES U.S.
IN SOVIET BREAKUP

"Why do you think it's boring?" I asked.

"Because it all seems so important," she answered.

It was perhaps the best, most direct definition of boring I'd ever heard. I roared with laughter. "You're right!" I told her. "It is important. It's the most important historical event to happen in your lifetime, and it's all laid out for you here on the pages of this paper. You get to see it before it gets to the history books. This is history in the making."

Finally I saw the look that I'd waited for during the yeast oratory — the head slightly tilted, the eyes widened in a minor degree of inquisitiveness. She didn't get it exactly, but she wanted to; she wanted to understand what the big deal was. I looked down at the paper myself. This was a critical moment. Was it possible to distill seventy-five years of Soviet history there on the spot so that my thirteen-year-old could grasp the significance of the morning's headlines, or would I induce an irreversible state of boredom?

I said, "If you allow me a sentence or two, I'll try to explain why this is all so important."

Charitably, she said, "You can take more if you need it."

I felt very Lithuanian at that moment — practically home free. I launched into a twenty-minute dissertation on the rise and fall of Soviet communism. I talked about the revolt against the rule of the czars, the coming to power of the Bolsheviks, the inevitable corruption of power. I told her about the hydrogen bomb, the Cuban missile crisis — when all the kids in my school thought we were going to be blown up at any moment — and the shifting alliances of war and peace. I found myself lapsing into Mr. Rogerspeak: Russia was our friend during World War II; after the war it became our enemy, and Germany, which had been our enemy, became our friend. And then Gorbachev came along and he wanted to be friends with everybody.

They would've wiped the floor with me for talk like that on *The McLaughlin Group,* but I could tell I was getting through to Gillian by the questions she started to ask: "If Gorbachev's a communist and the coup guys were communist, why did they try to throw him out? How come the guys in the tank didn't kill Yeltsin when he climbed on top of one of them? What's the difference between Gorbachev and Yeltsin?"

It was history in the making all right, personal as well as global. Two hours into our adventure, and Gillian had become a participant. We continued our survey:

THREE CURRENT, 2 EX-DEPUTIES
ACCUSED OF THEFT

"No taxes, Dad," she said, reacting to the alleged malfeasance of public employees.

FBI OPENS PROBE OF 3 SLAYINGS
BY SHERIFF'S DEPUTIES

"I mean it, Dad," she vowed. "I'm not paying taxes."

We discussed the placement of ads pitched to women in the lifestyle section (underwear, plastic surgery, weight loss programs); the placement of ads pitched to men in the sports section (tires, computers, female mud wrestlers); and high-end ads in the business section (jumbo CDs, Jaguars, estate auctions). We looked at the stock tables and planned on following a stock, which she would theoretically own, through the months ahead. When she asked how you gained and lost money in the market, I said I'd rather explain the rise and fall of communism again. She said she wanted to buy stock in Disney, so I described how Disney's stock had risen in recent years because of new management and warned her that it might lose ground again if the management changed again.

She was undaunted. "Dad," she said, "there's always going to be a Disneyland." Merrill Lynch couldn't have put it better.

It was Gillian who pointed out that it was 11:45, fifteen minutes beyond our appointed break time. I took it as a positive sign that she'd been patient and hadn't pointed out the time at 11:15. I was both relieved and satisfied with the way the morning had gone. As we made our way indoors, I tried to read her feelings in her body language, but reading my VCR's manual would have been easier. She was moving quickly in order to meet her friends at Redwood Junior High for lunch.

As I got ready to leave for work, I was thoroughly distracted by the unasked question. Because I was not going to open the door to negativity, I couldn't ask her directly how she felt. It was like the old story about the lady or the tiger: I wanted to know what was behind the door, but I feared being devoured by it. Describing the front page of the *L.A. Times* as boring was one thing — even comical — but if I'd asked and she'd described our first morning as boring, I may have had severe problems facing our second morning.

On my way out the door, I noticed her journal on the corner of the kitchen counter. I'd assigned her to write in it each day, saying that I'd check on it at random in the course of the year. She wasn't obliged to write in it until the end of her daily studies, but in my eagerness for clues, I picked it up anyway. Despite her haste to get to her friends, she had indeed recorded her reaction:

SEPTEMBER 5
Interesting, very interesting. It may take a while to get used to this new life style, but I'm tough. I think I can do it. I expected a little less the first day. But my brain isn't to

overworked.* I just hope the teacher remembers that I'm not a high school girl. Just 8th grade, and scince [*sic*] I didn't learn anything last year (except from my wonderful social studies teacher) or the year before that, I have a lot of basic catching up to do.
Let's try not 2 push it, DAD.

Well, it wasn't a five-star review, and the spelling needed work, but it was a good beginning — or so it seemed.

---

*For the reader's sake, Gillian's spelling is corrected throughout most of this book, except where misspellings help make a point or convey the idiosyncratic nature of teen English. The home school approach to bad spelling is dealt with later in detail.

4

CLASS SCHEDULE

HERE ARE the classes I unveiled for Gillian that first day:

	Monday	Tuesday	Wednesday	Thursday	Friday
7:30	Homemaking — make bed, clean room, make up for the day,* breakfast.				
8:00	Keeping up with The Times — looking at the world through the newspaper →				
8:30					
9:00	Math (numbers, logic & puzzles)	Discuss history	Discuss science	Review writing	Geography
9:30				Library time	Discuss film
10:00					
	Music	Discuss reading	Discuss reading		
10:30					
11:00					
11:30	LUNCH			Film (Romeo & Juliet; To Sir, With Love; Gandhi; The Miracle Worker; Jesus of Nazareth; Inherit the Wind; I Remember Mama; others)	Art class (later Lorna's class, and then a series of improvisations)
12:00	History study	Science study	Writing		
1:00					
1:30					
2:00					
	Novel reading	Novel reading			
2:30					
3:00					

*I allowed time for Gillian to do her make-up each morning, but alas, with no other males around to impress other than me, she abandoned the use of make-up immediately and later counted it among the foremost benefits of home schooling.

Before getting into details about each class, a few observations are in order.

First, the overriding idea was to allow Gillian and me to interact as teacher and student in the mornings and then for her to pursue an independent course of study in the afternoons, while I was at work. I encouraged her to call me at the office if she ran into any trouble on her own. On good days she would; on bad days she would show an unusual concern about interrupting me and just skip the assignment. Most days, fortunately, I did my job in leaving her with clearly defined assignments, and she did hers in completing them.

Second, this schedule, like that of ordinary teachers, does not reflect preparation time. I was most reminded of my prior teaching days in the evenings, when I would be up late creating lesson plans. The fear of facing a class unprepared, a residue of my teaching days, resurfaced, even though my class only had one student — my own daughter.

Third, I relied a good deal on visual media through the year. (I use the term to include movies, in theaters and on video; TV programming; and original videotape presentations.) Part of this reliance was pragmatic: it made short- and long-term scheduling so much easier. Gauging how long it would take Gillian to get through a two-hour film or a twelve-week video series was easier than gauging how long she would need to write a paper or read a book. Moreover, this reliance was grounded in my own educational philosophy, and I was happy to find validation for it early in the year. Tom Apostal, a professor of mathematics at Caltech, explaining his work as director of Project MATHEMATICS, a video series for teaching math to eighth- through twelfth-graders, wrote in the *L.A. Times:*

The power of visual images to stir the deepest emotions has always been understood by artists. Television places these images in motion together with music and special effects. Its impact on the human mind is well understood by entertainers, advertisers and politicians, but not, it seems, by most educators. Instead of blaming TV, let's exploit this technology creatively . . . to young people. Let's bring quality television into the classroom as a powerful visual aid to be used together with books, computers and supplementary materials.

The operative word in that quotation, for me, was *quality*. Like books, visual media range from art to trash. As with literature, my job as Gillian's parent — her educator — would be to help her learn to discriminate between the two.

Raising children with television in the house, we had made one attempt at censorship. During Meagan's childhood, we wouldn't allow her to watch *Three's Company* in prime time because of what appeared to be a rather moronic treatment of sex. By the time Gillian reached the same age, *Three's Company* was in syndication, so it had oozed out of its time slot and was all over the TV dial and the clock. To maintain our censorship would have required eternal vigilance or throwing out the TV altogether. We concluded that it was far wiser to begin the process of teaching her to discriminate between good and bad TV than to choose for her and attempt to enforce it.

For me, that discriminating process runs on two tracks. The first is to point out consistently and reasonably the failings of objectionable programs. The second is to provide quality alternatives. The first track was always easy enough to run. I'd simply walk into the TV room, take a brief but disapproving stance in front of whatever stupid show was on at the time, and say something like, "Have the Bundys done their toilet joke yet?" After three or four shots like that, the reasonably intelligent child begins to see the predictability of such things and moves on to other offerings — if not always better ones. Naturally, exposing Gillian in adolescence to some of the good alternatives available was sometimes like leading a pony to water. Actually getting her to drink some of that good-for-you programming proved to be one of the great subsidiary benefits of the home school.

Inasmuch as visual media, and television in particular, are still a largely passive experience, lessons in them are not always self-evident, no matter how high the quality. That's why I planned never to allow a visually driven assignment to stand alone. Gillian would always be required to take notes in response to study questions, and our subsequent discussions, tests, or essays would depend on her notes. No matter what the subject, whenever we used visual media Gillian could not simply watch it and then switch off; she had to think about what she'd seen.

Thursdays, 1–3 p.m., Movies. My very first parent-teacher confrontation was over Franco Zeffirelli's production of *Romeo and Juliet*. Even before its release, the film had attracted considerable attention on two counts. One was Zeffirelli's choice of two very young, untried actors for the lead roles; the other was the scant nudity he'd allowed. Before we saw the film, the parents of my seventh-to-ninth-graders demanded a meeting with me — and it wasn't to discuss casting. They had not seen the movie, of course (people rarely do in these cases), but they had heard that it provided a tantalizing glimpse of young Leonard Whiting's behind.

I tried to explain that this version of the classic love story was specifically aimed at providing young audiences with a palatable introduction to Shakespeare. The parents were not persuaded — most of them, anyway. A few allowed their children to see the movie, but the majority fell in line behind a red-faced she-lion who shouted at me in the midst of our meeting, "You'll feel differently about this when you have children of your own!"

It was, perhaps, in memory of that mother that I scheduled *Romeo and Juliet* as the first film Gillian would watch at the Dan Riley School for a Girl. I had checked it out of the library and left it with her while I went to work.

Meagan and Lorna were there to greet me when I got home that evening, with Meagan reporting that she'd come home from college that afternoon to find Gillian crying uncontrollably in the den. My blood instantly chilled, then just as instantly warmed as Meagan explained. "It was *Romeo and Juliet*. She was crying over the movie." The three of us looked at one another and shared a smile, acknowledging our mutual deduction that Gillian had just taken a step toward womanhood.

Gillian, who had always been generous with her tears for animals, had never been known to cry for any human being in a movie. I never begrudged the animals the sympathy, but I was always dismayed that Gillian could fret so freely over an animal in distress, yet watch dispassionately while countless human beings were maimed, tortured, and killed. At long last, here were tears for humanity from Gillian.

Without any prompting from me, her feelings made their way into her journal: "Never do I think I have felt so much or cried for any movie as *Romeo and Juliet*. Truly one of the best movies ever made. Not only the wonderful story, but the actors. I just don't know how to explain it. I wasn't involved in the true words — otherwise I would have been completely lost. But the story itself just took me away. I didn't realize a story could be so powerful. I hope I never have to see this in high school. Otherwise I better buy a lot of waterproof mascara."

I was jubilant. It seemed I had struck a rich new vein of compassion in Gillian with my very first choice of a film.

Or maybe not. Maybe we — her family — had suddenly seen a side of Gillian that we had missed before. I didn't really know. At that moment, in fact, I didn't even know that I didn't know. But clearly the process of education had begun — for both teacher and student.

Fridays, 9–10 a.m., Geography. Not terribly high on my list of concerns about Gillian, but on the list nonetheless, was whether she knew where Mexico and Canada were. A recent survey of American high school students had revealed that an alarming number of them didn't know. So that was the first question I asked Gillian when we met for our first geography lesson: Do you know where Canada and Mexico are? I was greatly relieved when she looked at me as if I were an idiot, then promptly pointed out the two giant neighbors on the map before us.

We were back in the gazebo again, and a pattern was being established that would hold for most of the school term: breakfast together over the newspaper at the kitchen counter, and then out under the warmth of the sun for lessons on the picnic table.

Fortunately, because the "where's Mexico and Canada" lesson was so brief, we were able to follow up on the previous day's discussion of the breakup of the Soviet empire. Looking at the map, one could almost build a case for students' woeful performance in geography. According to *National Geo-*

graphic, the world map is being remade constantly — six times in a twelve-month period during 1991 and 1992. And there on the map in front of us was yet another new world order for them to learn. In the past twenty-four hours, or thereabouts, eighteen countries had emerged — or reemerged — from the Soviet Union.

God bless the child who chooses to be a geographer. That would probably not be my child; although Gillian surprised me with a real facility for reading maps. And it was during one of our subsequent geography lessons that she came up with her boldest initiative vis-à-vis home schooling. My focus in all our geography lessons was on places of immediate relevance: this is where Russia is; this is where Romeo and Juliet lived; this is where your sister was born. When we came to locating her grandparents' ancestral homes, she was inspired. Let's go on a field trip, she suggested — and she wasn't talking about those ancestral homes in Connecticut and Massachusetts either. I got so caught up in her enthusiasm that I immediately committed us to a European field trip later in the year, thus increasing the operating budget of the Dan Riley School for a Girl considerably.

Fridays, 1–3 p.m., Art. The fluidity of my schedule first exhibited itself in art class. My tenure as Gillian's art teacher did not last beyond the first two weeks. I admit to being worthless in art for drawing anything more complex than some rudimentary stick figures, so I planned to focus the course on the history of art. But Gillian had shown some talent in art over the years, so Lorna enrolled her in a community art class in the interest of keeping the talent alive and well under a real art teacher.

It was not a success. Gillian did not like the teacher, and the feeling seemed to be mutual. Meagan had also signed up for the class, more or less to keep Gillian company, and thus became the first member of the family to observe Gillian in a classroom setting. "I don't know what it is," she reported, "but this teacher really seems to be afraid of her. He never looks her in the eye when he talks to her about her work, and when he does talk to her about her work, he has much less to say to her than to anyone else in the class."

Among the many facets of Gillian's personality, bubbliness is not one that springs to mind. If one, particularly an adult, is going to have a successful relationship with Gillian, one is going to have to scale the walls of her natural reserve and wariness. Some adults are afraid of such heights. I concluded that her art teacher was one of them.

Mondays, 9–10:30 a.m., Math. Admittedly, our schedule had some odd features to it, teaching math just once a week being a major one. I believe there's a considerable body of evidence that suggests that it should be done every day in order to have a cumulative effect on the student. Had a primary goal of the home schooling been to make Gillian a better math student, I would have taken that into consideration. But I had a nagging suspicion that math could be the main academic source of contention between us, so I tried to minimize it from the beginning.

In their book, the Colfaxes had revealed the same humanities bias as I have, and they had warned that the choices of math texts for home teaching were meager. Therefore I'd gone about my search for resources with modest expectations. If there had been a textbook that was magically going to unlock the mysteries of mathematics for children taught at home, it was unlikely that the country would be facing the crisis that John Allen Poulos called innumeracy in his book of the same name. So I followed my basic educational instinct that achievement in math, like everything else, was based on a state of mind, meaning that a positive state would yield positive results. I hoped that Poulos's book, along with *Aha* and *Gotcha* by Martin Gardner of *Scientific American,* would help instill a sense of fun into our math lessons.

We kicked off our study of math with a TV show, a one-hour PBS special on classroom math featuring a former L.A. math teacher, Jaime Gallante, of *Stand and Deliver* fame. Gallante's power in reaching his students, it seemed to me, was based on the three essentials of effective teaching: knowing the subject well, keeping the students' focus on the subject, and communicating the subject to the students clearly. Watching Gillian's eyes, wide and intent as the show unfolded, persuaded me that it would have been worth sitting through a month of PBS pledge breaks to turn that program into a twenty-eight-week series.

As it turned out, my fears about problems arising over math were sadly borne out. One of the rules I had made at the outset was that there would be no comparisons between the home school and the public school — as in: "This isn't how we did it last year." Gillian followed that rule fairly well except in math and except when she was feeling frustrated about the subject at hand or the general course of her life. Then she'd hit me with a barrage of confidence shakers, such as: "We already learned this at Redwood last year," or "They haven't even started doing this at Redwood yet," or "My teacher last year took more time to explain this," or "This book is dumb."

To make matters worse, we had what was clearly our biggest academic fiasco over math. One day I would follow up a particularly fruitless lesson on percentages by taking her through the newspaper and showing her how often percentages were used. We came to a typical ad for shoes — *Up to*

33% off! I asked Gillian to figure out the new price on a pair of these shoes. She did just as I had been trying to teach her, subtracting the new price from the old and dividing into the difference. When she was done, she came up with a figure a few dollars less than the advertised price. I checked her division with a calculator. She was right. What we had in front of us was a clear case of false advertising, and it called for action, so we fired up the computer and issued a sharp consumer letter to the shoe store.

This was education as I idealized it — the integration of multiple disciplines and the mobilization of an informed and concerned community of citizen/consumers. I imagined the Dan Riley School for a Girl prominently featured on *60 Minutes*. We would dutifully hand our calculations over to Mike Wallace, who would then expose the deviousness of the shoe store owner, who would vainly try to hide his shame behind a rack of ladies' pumps. As it turned out, however, the only thing exposed was my own stupidity. A week later, a curt reply from the shoe store indicated the error of our math. I had indeed checked Gillian's division, but I had never checked her subtraction, and it had been wrong.

This was an embarrassment that begged to be buried. After all, only Gillian and I knew about it. I'm compelled to relate it here for two reasons, however. The first is that if it had gone the other way, it would have made a terrific anecdote and I would have been trumpeting it far and wide. The second, and more important, is that learning to own up to one's errors, I believe, is as much a part of a good education as learning one's math. If Gillian ended up engaged in the current mania for pointing fingers, I wanted to be sure that she got plenty of practice on herself.

Mondays, 10:30–11:30 a.m., Music. As with the art class,

my plans for our Monday morning music class never really took flight. As conceived, it was going to be the hour each week devoted to an appreciation of Bach, Mozart, Beethoven, et al. But on the very first day I suffered a peculiar loss of nerve and reverted instead to "The Rock 'n' Roll Textbook," which had emerged from a class I'd taught years earlier, exploring various social and ethical issues through rock lyrics. Somehow I thought that I'd be overplaying my hand if I sat Gillian down and asked her to start identifying things like the first movement of Beethoven's Fifth. In something of a panic, I decided we'd best make our way back to the classics through the works of Mr. Bob Dylan, the Beatles, Joni Mitchell, et al. We never did get to classical music, though, and I comfort myself with the thought that I may have given Gillian a longer-term appreciation of it by that failure.

Mondays, 1–2 p.m., and Tuesdays, 9–10:30 a.m., History. Outside a war was raging over school curriculum, especially in regard to history, and the Dan Riley School for a Girl was not entirely insulated from it. Would Gillian get a multicultural view of history or a Eurocentric one? Would we focus on the role of women in history? Or gays? Or God? If I had been driven by some ideological agenda, choosing our direction would have been simpler. I could have opened the little red book of whatever doctrine I'd bought for myself and taught Gillian from it. But mine was a most determinedly nonideological outlook. Not only was I skeptical about almost all bodies of dogma, I even had questions about the most routine matters of education. For instance, what is knowledge?

In the introduction to his book on England's Wars of the Roses, John Gillingham observes that generations of supposedly educated Englishmen went out into the world secure in their knowledge of those wars as they had learned it from Shakespeare. But Gillingham contends that all those Eton lads and Oxford grads couldn't have had a more unreliable source for their understanding, for Shakespeare had simply created an intoxicating mix of errant history and brilliant drama for future empire builders to imbibe. Were they then intelligent because they knew their Shakespeare, or were they ignorant because they knew their history from Shakespeare and he was wrong?

The obvious assumption may be that we in the modern world have a more reliable handle on knowledge than Shakespeare did. But while the Dan Riley School for a Girl was in session, Oliver Stone's film *JFK* was released, dramatically raising the question again of what is known and what is known that is really false. After seeing the movie, Meagan suggested that I put it on the list of films for Gillian to see, but I declined. I wasn't at all squeamish about teaching her from a movie that featured the bare bottom of a teenage actor, nor did I shrink from teaching her about the cruelty of slavery from *Roots* or the horrors of Nazism from *The Diary of Anne Frank*. And Gillian was free to watch *JFK* herself if she wanted — as a movie. But as a history lesson *JFK*, like *Henry IV*, was too speculative and hysterical for my syllabus.

When gossip and propaganda pass for history, it becomes less useful as a guide to times past and more a barometer of what appeases tastes and attitudes in our own time. Judging by the national headlines, math may have been the subject that aroused the greatest sense of inadequacy, but history was the one that aroused the greatest emotional debate. My own inner conflict was mild compared to the one that raged in certain public school districts where the question of true historical knowledge was being viewed through a kaleidoscope of factious racial, ethnic, and cultural biases. In my small domain, I simply had to avoid being so paralyzed by the question of what was and was not true historical knowledge that I set Gillian adrift on a sea of uncertainties. I also wanted to avoid being so doctrinaire about what it was that she became like little Soviet scholars of the past seventy years who had demonstrated wisdom by mastering state lies.

I ended up choosing Alistair Cooke's PBS series *America* as the basis of our history course. It probably leaned more to the standard-issue, white male's view of American history. But I felt that whatever bias was betrayed by Cooke's race or sex was balanced by a deep respect for both the U.S. Constitution and the audience's powers of discernment. That was reliable enough for me, so I entrusted Gillian's history instruction to Alistair Cooke each Monday afternoon, supplemented by a long list of study questions I devised, which we would then discuss each Tuesday morning.

Mondays and Tuesdays, 2–3 p.m.; Tuesdays and Wednesdays 10:30–11:30 a.m., Novel Reading. I called this part of the schedule Novel Reading, but it was a misnomer. Two of the four books we undertook during the year were not novels. Devoting four time slots to it, compared to one for math, further exposed my own humanities bias and wasn't at all warranted by any objective evaluation of Gillian's strengths and weaknesses. She had always tested extremely well in reading comprehension and vocabulary, so I was clearly teaching from my strength to hers, in this regard, and can't really justify it pedagogically. But I saw our reading of books together as an opportunity to explore values and attitudes, which was a high priority of the home school. Besides, despite her fine performance as a reader in the past, Gillian, like so many of her peers, did not ordinarily walk around with her nose in a book. I hoped that our reading together would inspire her to read more on her own.

Tuesdays, 1–2 p.m., and Wednesdays, 9–10:30 a.m., Science. David Attenborough's terrific PBS series, *The Living Planet,* which explored the living organisms of the sea, the earth, and the air, formed the basis of our science curriculum. Gillian had a general enthusiasm for natural science born of her intense interest in animals, especially horses, so I tried to enlist that enthusiasm by reversing our roles from the *America* series. Gillian would make up study questions to lead me through the follow-up discussion. That meant she would watch the video first; then I would watch it, accompanied by her questions. It was just a tantalizing taste of Postman and Weingartner's student question approach to learning. Again, another time, another circumstance, and we would have had a full buffet of it.

Wednesday, 1–3 p.m., Writing. The writing assignments covered a wide range of subjects. One of the earliest generated my favorite paper of the entire year. It came from one of those Monday morning "Rock 'n' Roll Textbook" discussions and was based on "Julie through the Glass," an old Carly Simon song that hints at reincarnation. In the paper Gillian wrote:

> I believe I have had past lives before. As a matter of fact, I'm almost positive of it because I remember having this exact same assignment once before.
>
> I was a junior in high school in Dan Riley's English class. I can swear we got this same assignment.
>
> My best friends, Flowers & Peace, always ditched school, but this was the one class we stayed for.
>
> Our teacher was so neato. He was one of the few who didn't say anything about our groovy clothes and our hip-

pie-parted, greasy hair styles. We loved studying songs and their meanings. It was the only class we didn't mind going to.

Now here I am in a similar situation with Mr. Riley as my teacher, but this time he's also my dad. I wonder if we'll meet up again in another lifetime, perhaps doing the same thing. It happens a lot. People everywhere are meeting up again in another lifetime. I know because I've seen the movie *Dead Again.*

The paper reminded me of my best days as a teacher, days when I could elicit funny, freewheeling papers, full of the wacky kinds of insights and truths only kids can sometimes see.

Thursdays, 10–11:30 a.m., Library. Our initial curriculum was rounded out by regular trips to the library. Having grown up in a home with few books, I developed an early and deep appreciation for libraries, so I wanted Gillian, my anti-tax daughter, to fully understand the generosity a culture expresses when it builds libraries.

As we made our way to the library for the first time as teacher and student, I told her about the little library across the street from my childhood home. It was even smaller than the one in the house Gillian's been raised in, but it still contained wonders that could lift an imagination right out of a milltown with the mere flick of a page. I told her that back then the most wondrous book of all was a big, colorfully illustrated book of Bible stories that gave dramatic life to the Scripture readings we'd hear every Sunday in church: Noah's ark casting about in the flood, Daniel in the lion's den, David taking on Goliath.

I did not tell her, however, that for me the most compelling of all those pictures was of Adam and Eve being driven from the Garden. I had a boyish infatuation with Eve, racing away from God's wrath in her shamed but still sensuous nakedness: Lust inspired in a young boy's heart by the holiest book of all — best kept secret from impressionable young daughters.

I told her that libraries were often victims of righteous crusades by those who wanted to purge them of what they considered unwholesome material. Censorship is a hot button with Gillian. As a member of the MTV generation, she's very keen on First Amendment rights, but I thought she should know that writers have fought those battles long before rock stars ever did, many of them through libraries.

I did not want Gillian to see our first visit to the library in terms of her past school trips — a search through musty shelves for research materials. There would be plenty of time for that later in the year. I wanted this to be a near religious experience, so with Gillian cloistered in my car, I launched into a sermon about how libraries speak of a culture's respect for its past, its faith in its future, and its dedication to seeking truth. And I told her that libraries needed friends and supporters from her generation or all of that could be lost someday. Indeed, in the course of the home school year, our town library, a source of enormous civic pride, was forced to close its doors on Fridays, double its late fees, levy a $55 annual fee on users from out of town, and lay off fifteen employees. The most important library lesson for Gillian would be: Don't take it for granted.

There was no physical education on the schedule. Gillian's needs in that area would be met by horseback riding and soccer. She rode on a neighborhood horse, KC, in exchange for caring for him. She played soccer for an AYSO league team, which, in keeping with the theme of the year, I insisted she join. This really did mark a break from our prior approach to raising Gillian — and Meagan, for that matter. Lorna and I had generally been inclined to let the girls make their own choices, but Gillian's disappointing choices steadily pushed me toward making more and more decisions for her. During one of her soccer games, I had that excruciating parental experience of overhearing another parent evaluate my child in public. He was not the typical loudmouth, who shows up at kids' games to work out his own aggressions, but a knowledgeable guy whose English accent created the impression that he knew more about the game than the coaches — which, as the winless season dragged on, may have been the case. "Number 9! Number 9!" he was yelling, trying to position Gillian more effectively on defense. Gillian, beyond hearing or caring, ignored him. He sat down, shaking his head and muttering, "She's such a talented player if she'd only keep her head in the game." I stood off to the side, juggling conflicting reactions. Should I go up and introduce myself and thank him for recognizing Gillian's talent, or did I invite him to engage in fisticuffs under the stands for daring to question my daughter's intensity? In the end I did neither. English accent and all, it'd been a pretty astute assessment of my little girl.

A hallmark of our schedule was its fluidity. I had hoped, of course, that I had done a good enough job so that most of the schedule would survive the year, but I took great comfort in knowing that if a class or lesson within a class was ill conceived in any way, I had the freedom to change. From the beginning, then, I was prepared to alter things that weren't working (the music and art) and to add things that might enhance the whole experience. One week, for instance, we had Katalin, an Australian exchange student, living with us, and for a few days she tutored Gillian in the geography, history, and culture of Down Under. Another time, our viewing of *Roots* led us to spin off a genealogy unit, and for a few weeks Gillian corresponded with her grandparents about ancestral data for a family tree.

The most deliberate later addition to the schedule was Lorna. She would have been part of it from the first bell if I had not insisted otherwise. But I did so for numerous reasons. One was for Lorna's own good. She was running her own company, creating and giving business seminars all over the West, and already worked exceedingly long hours. She would never have begged out of participating in the school (she never begs out of anything), and I was growing increasingly concerned about her overly taxed resources.

Another was for Gillian's good. Although Lorna and I agreed completely on the need to affect the direction of Gillian's life, we did not agree about what to do, as Lorna's initial objections to the home school indicated. I thought it was important that Gillian see the foundation of the home school go down firmly in order to take it seriously, and I believed that effort could be undermined by procedural debates between Lorna and me, no matter how well intended.

The third reason was for my own good. With all my concern for Gillian's development as a student and citizen, my underlying concern was with our relationship as father and daughter. I believed it had reached a low point in her seventh-grade year, and I wasn't optimistic about its getting better. I saw the home schooling as a last good chance for us to rectify our relationship. I didn't think Lorna needed this experience with Gillian as much as I did. Her relationship with Gillian was not burdened by nightmares, anxieties, and diabolical plans for transforming her life in a crazed, fright-filled evening. A single story, in fact, best illustrates the differences between us.

The previous year, Gillian had begged us to waive the usual single-guest limit for a sleepover. She wanted three or four, although it may as well have been fifty as far as I was concerned. I raised my usual protest against the noise, the mess, the general disruption of domestic tranquillity. Gillian, with Lorna's support, prevailed. I, with human nature on my side, was in line for the last laugh when, sometime between one and two in the morning, Lorna and I were both awakened by a loud ruckus coming from the site of the sleepover. Lorna was disgruntled; I was in a satisfying rage. All my worst prophecies about the evening were unfolding. I was hopping around the darkened bedroom, trying to get into the pants I would be wearing as I dropped each girl off at her own home. But before I could huff and puff and blow the sleepover to kingdom come, Lorna was in her robe and making her way down the hall with a word over her shoulder that I should relax; she would handle it. I fell back onto the bed, muttering about the scourge of our time — softness — softness on communism, softness on crime, softness on children. And then came the ever so soft, lilting tones of Pachelbel's "Canon" — Lorna on the piano. The demons in my soul started to yawn and curl up for the evening as the girls at the other end of the house were treated to one of the rarest privileges in life after infancy — a lullaby.

With a touch like that available, I would have been an idiot to deny Lorna's participation in the home schooling for long, and that was never my intention. Once the foundation was laid, Lorna, who had already taken Gillian to a number of seminars before the home school, would present a course of her own. Before that, however, Lorna took her to a local appearance by the famed physicist Stephen Hawking. We didn't think there was a chance in the world that Gillian would understand a word he had to say about the history of time, but we thought it would be a rare and valuable opportunity for her to be in the presence of greatness, however tangentially. When Lorna was Gillian's age, she'd met Ernest Hemingway — in a swimming pool, of all places. She hadn't known who he was and had read none of his books, but later in life she experienced the profound realization that she'd had contact with one of the giants of the age. Perhaps through this fleeting contact with Hawking, we thought that Gillian, too, might one day be able to measure the manufactured, transient celebrity that litters the landscape against the true genius that transforms it.

One day, perhaps, but not soon. Lorna had been exhilarated to watch Hawking, in defiance of the disease that confined him to a wheelchair and robbed him of speech, methodically respond to questions on a keyboard; the result was then broadcast to the audience through a computerized voice box. But Gillian expressed immense frustration with the entire event and announced, "I'm never going to another seminar as long as I live!"

Her children, we hoped, might one day hear a happier version of that day.

When we were only halfway through the schedule for the first week, Gillian was ready with an assessment in her journal, hopeful, no doubt, that it would fall into the right hands:

SEPTEMBER 9
I think my head is getting too big. Not because my ego is getting larger, but because my head is getting too much information. I think my days should only go to 11:30 every day cuz that's already 4 hours of straight learning and 3 times as much as any normal person would learn per day!

That way we wouldn't have to worry about my head ex-
ploding! Especially since I don't get any vacations.
I don't know how you talked me into this. You tricked
me! I know I'm learning too much. Don't try to hide it!

That entry revealed a lot about Gillian — her strong satiri-
cal bent for one; that troublesome tic she experienced when
adding and subtracting (the 4 hours of straight learning she
was referring to really didn't begin until 8 A.M., making for
3 ½ hours of head-endangerment), and finally her mastery of
what is called in sales the presumptive close. That business
about no vacations was her idea. She wanted to waive all
rights to vacations during home schooling so that she could
get out early and return to Redwood in time to take part in the
junior high graduation ceremonies with her pals. Although I
had clearly discouraged the idea (for the good of both of us)
and it had not even been discussed with officials at Redwood,
there she was, four days into her journal, talking as if it were a
fait accompli — and using it as a bargaining chip, no less! It
was quintessential Gillian.

5

THE FIRST QUARTER

I THINK OF OUR FIRST QUARTER as the Anne Frank quarter. Having never actually read *The Diary of Anne Frank,* I had always thought of it strictly as a Holocaust story. I had no idea that it was a story about growing up as well, rich in timeless insights into female adolescence. I chose it as the first book Gillian and I would read together simply because it was by a teenage girl. I also liked the idea that it was historical rather than contemporary. The daily newspaper would give us all the conversation we needed about that ubiquitous trinity of teen topics — sex, drugs, and suicide. World war and genocide, I thought, might give Gillian an appreciation of some teenage problems that weren't quite so self-absorbing.

Great books, however, wield their own power — and on their own terms. Anne Frank's diary would ultimately succeed, not so much as a primer for Gillian of a world at war, but as a primer for me of a girl at war with a world where adults appear to ration fun, love, and understanding according to their own relentless timetables. The shock of recognizing my daughter on the pages of Anne Frank's diary was profound. Two girls born fifty years apart on two different continents under two entirely different sets of circumstances, and yet . . .

Am I really so bad mannered, conceited, headstrong, pushing, stupid, lazy, etc., etc. as they all say? Oh, of course not. I have my faults just like everyone else, I know that, but they thoroughly exaggerate everything.

       — Anne Frank's diary, September 28, 1942

Sometimes I wonder if I will ever understand this world and the crazy people who live in it. Sometimes I like to sit back and pretend I'm invisible and watch the world go. I laugh at the silly things people do, the way they act. Yet, when I am not in this frame of mind, I act just like them — making silly mistakes and acting in a foolish manner.

    I have been very observant in the last month or so, watching the way people act. Although I do not understand it, I am able to communicate with them better. I believe this is why I'm getting along better with everyone.

       — Gillian's journal, October 4, 1991

Honestly, you needn't think it's easy to be the "badly brought up" central figure of a hypercritical family in hiding. When I lie in bed at night and think over the many sins and shortcomings attributed to me, I get so confused by it all that I either laugh or cry; it depends on what sort of mood I'm in.

       — Anne Frank's diary, November 28, 1942

I didn't write for so long because there was nothing really to write about. But now I find myself with so much to say. I shall have to spread it out over a few days.

    I was wondering how long we were going to go without fights between the teacher/father and student/daughter. Well, I got my answer — two months, which is pretty good. I didn't think it would last this long.

    Bickering is such a childish thing. I think it is somehow

necessary, otherwise people wouldn't do it so often. It is full
of childishness when it is over stupid things like it has been
lately. We fight less, but over stupider things.

— Gillian's journal, November 4, 1991

. . . [I]f I talk everyone thinks I'm showing off; when I'm
silent they think I'm ridiculous; rude if I answer; sly if I get
a good idea, lazy if I'm tired, selfish if I eat a mouthful more
than I should, stupid, cowardly, crafty, etc. etc. The whole
day long I hear nothing else but that I am an insufferable
baby, and although I laugh about it and pretend not to take
any notice, I do mind. I would like to ask God to give me
a different nature so I didn't put everyone's back up. But
that can't be done.

— Anne Frank's diary, January 30, 1943

Every second I'm with my friends is valuable to me now. I
take care of each one. I don't think the time we spend
together is as important to my friends as it is to me. I
thought my only real friend was B so I shut everyone else
out. But they have proved me wrong. They do care. I have
found that accepting them and their faults has helped me
to enjoy life much more. Maybe I've even taken a little hell
out of their lives. Who knows?

— Gillian's journal, October 7, 1991

I'm awfully scared that everyone who knows me as I am
will discover that I have another side, a finer, better side.
Sometimes if I really compel the good Anne to take the
stage for a quarter of an hour, she simply shrivels up as
soon as she has to speak, and lets Anne number one take
over, and before I realize it she has disappeared.

. . . [T]he nice Anne is never present in company, has not
appeared one single time so far, but almost always pre-

dominates when we're alone . . . I've acquired the name of chaser after boys, flirt, know-all . . . The cheerful Anne laughs about it, gives cheeky answers, shrugs her shoulders indifferently, behaves as if she doesn't care, but . . . the quiet Anne's reactions are just the opposite. . . . I must admit that it does hurt me, that I try terribly hard to change myself, but I'm always fighting against a more powerful enemy.

> — Anne Frank's diary, August 1, 1944

I feel like the most confused person in the world. I feel I am changing so much in every way. My whole personality is swirling around. I can't wait to see what comes out of all this. One day I want to kill every one in sight. Other days I feel like I'm M. L. King, Gandhi, Kennedy, and Eleanor Roosevelt.

See, I told you I was confused.

> — Gillian's journal, January 21, 1992

Gillian recognized her kinship with Anne Frank almost immediately, and early in her reading said, only half in jest, "I think I'm Anne Frank reincarnated." This feeling reverberated as we got deeper into the book, and I began to see not only Gillian but close to a mirror image of our entire family. The surface similarity was obvious, of course. The Franks, like the Rileys, were a family with two daughters, one in her early teens, the other pushing adulthood. The relationship between mother and younger daughter could often be testy; the rivalry between siblings could sometimes be intense.

Occasionally the similarities were uncanny. A week after Gillian and I started a unit on genealogy to correspond to her seeing *Roots,* we came upon Anne studying genealogy. Then Anne described studying math with her father — a perfect portrait of Gillian and myself engaged in the same subject: "I flatly refuse to do these math problems every day," Anne wrote. "Daddy agrees that they're vile. I'm almost better at them than he is."

There was even an ill-considered letter that Anne wrote to her father (nicknamed Pim) that caused enormous hurt and misunderstanding between them: "Why is it that Pim annoys me? So much so that I can hardly bear him teaching me, that his affectionate ways strike me as being put on, that I want to be left in peace and would really prefer it if he dropped me a bit, until I felt more certain in my attitude toward him. Because I still have a gnawing feeling of guilt over that horrible letter I dared to write him . . ."

Finally there was the inescapable similarity between what Otto Frank had done, trying to hide his family from Hitler, and what I was trying to do with the home school. Nothing so horrifying as the Third Reich was marching outside our door, of course. Nonetheless, I recognized that, much as I wanted to deny it, I was still the naked father-warrior, patrolling the dark perimeter of my private nightmares, ever on guard against a motley crew of evils.

STUDY SHOWS A MILLION
TEEN SUICIDE ATTEMPTS

The morning that headline appeared, I asked Gillian why she thought so many teenagers committed suicide. "Because everything is wrong," she replied, "Everything."

"What do you mean by 'everything'?" I asked.

"Pollution," she said. "All we ever hear is how we're destroying the planet. No good water. No good air. No good anything. And someone's always telling you don't do this and don't do that because you'll get sick if you do, or you'll die.

And then you're walking down the street and there's always someone else asking you to do something, walking up to you and whispering in your ear." She put her hand to her mouth and mimicked pulling someone over to the side and asking them to buy. To *buy what* was left to my imagination, and I left it there. I didn't probe Gillian for details. I didn't want to get greedy. She was opening up to me more than ever before, and I was willing to read between the lines if that's what she wanted.

When she plaintively said, "You and Mommy have no idea how many times I have to say no when I'm out on my own," it nearly broke my heart. Not only didn't we have any idea, we didn't even think of Gillian as a kid who could or would say no. Lorna and I had always perceived her as a risk taker, a view that definitely influenced the formation of the home school. We didn't just want to stop the world for her, we wanted to know how it looked to her. Before the risks got greater in midadolescence, we needed to gain some assurance that she was aware of social dangers and capable of exercising caution. This comment two weeks into the school year was the first real indication we'd ever had that when she was out on her own, she knew enough to impose limits on her behavior. Although I was sad to realize how much pressure she was under, I was also relieved that she acknowledged those pressures rather than dismissing them as mere parental scare tactics, as she had in the past.

She had also spoken with a sense of urgency and anger I'd not previously heard from her on any subject that didn't relate to her personally. She'd casually expressed concern about global ills before, but never in rage. All those tired clichés about the kind of world we're leaving our children suddenly came roaring to life in front of me. Gillian's outburst suggested that the dreaded future that's been prophesied for decades is now upon us. It's there for our kids to see, big and plain, and there's no covering it up, no protecting them from it.

Still, I had to ask myself how accurate Gillian's assessment was of the rising number of suicides among the nation's young. Were kids really locking themselves in the family garage with the engine running because of the depleted ozone layer? Probably not, I guessed; not directly, anyway. But who knows what the cumulative effect of all the bad news is on a fragile, young psyche? It's clear that most kids are likely to be driven to the brink of suicide by very personal calamities — breaking up with a sweetheart, parental divorce, drug paranoia, and the like. But how do we know what they see when they look back from that brink? Perhaps a world seemingly run amok is just what tips the decision for them, convinces them that there is no salvation here?

I asked Gillian if she thought teenagers today really faced a world any more hostile than Romeo and Juliet's. I asked her to consider the parallels between teenage life in Shakespeare's Verona and 1990s America — gangs, violence, secret sex, and suicide. I thought maybe she wouldn't feel so sorry for her generation if she saw that centuries of human progress hadn't made much difference in teenage life; there had always been divisions into warring factions — from Capulets and Montagues to Bloods and Crips — along with the mindless bloodletting, the sex stolen in the night, and death as the ultimate refuge.

It was a good question to ask, but I realized its potential for even further despair if Gillian believed that the course of human events was basically confined to a treadmill, that no matter how we dressed up our lives, we were still going through the same motions as generations before us. But I let the question stand because I believe in historical perspective; I wanted Gillian to realize that her generation wasn't alone on a remote island in history — that there's precedent in and connection with all that has gone before. I think that perspective is the only way we answer the three central questions about ourselves as a species:

* is our movement forward, backward, or repetitious?
* do we have any real control over our movement?
* and if we do have control, how do we exercise it?

Gillian couldn't answer my question; it was too far in the past.

I then said, "Well, how about Anne Frank? She lived only fifty years ago. You don't know any teenagers who have had to put up with what she had to put up with, do you?"

She puzzled over the question briefly, then declared, "I have no idea." There was a note of finality that spoke volumes about her view of the question: I've got enough problems living in a world with drugs, AIDS, and drive-by shootings; don't ask me to imagine one with Adolf Hitler running around loose in it.

It is, of course, the problem with teaching history. *They've got their problems; I've got mine* is a familiar refrain from the human chorus, and it reaches a crescendo when the *they* in question are long dead and buried. From the beginning, I constantly tried to make Gillian trade off with the past, to understand how things got to be the way they are through historical process and how history itself is best understood through the prism of our own lives.

Gillian never really liked Alistair Cooke's *America* series. She found it boring; Cooke may be just a little too urbane for the typical thirteen-year-old. Yet the series helped frame some of our best discussions: every week, some historical issue from the series was resonating through our daily news. Cooke would recount the colonial tax revolts, and there we'd be, reading about some citizens who were protesting a "view tax" their town sought to levy against their ocean views. Cooke would describe the Constitutional Convention's struggle to create a bill of rights, guaranteeing the freedoms of speech and assembly and the right to bear arms, and there we'd be, hearing about the State of Florida cracking down on rap lyrics, the City of Los Angeles cracking down on gangs in city parks, and the rampant spread of guns in the nation's schools. Cooke would rhapsodize about the marvelous constitutional mechanism of checks and balances, and there we'd be, riveted to our TV during the confirmation hearings for Clarence Thomas. Sometimes it all seemed to dovetail so neatly that I could have sworn it had been planned.

As Gillian and I immersed ourselves in these issues, I was pleased to see the quality of our conversation improve. In our personal history, too much of it had been confined to commands and admonitions: Clean your room, do the dishes, do your homework, be off the phone in five minutes. Home schooling gave me the opportunity to open up entirely new areas of conversation with her. As I had been pleased to learn that she was capable of resisting temptation on the streets, I was doubly pleased to see that she actually had the makings of a very definite political philosophy in her head. She was a budding libertarian — a philosophy well suited to adolescence, I thought. She had that abiding contempt for taxes, and her reaction to the move to ban rap lyrics sounded like a libertarian battle cry: "If you don't like it, don't buy, don't watch, don't listen; just turn it off and walk away."

Interestingly, I reexamined and clarified my own political philosophy in my conversations with Gillian. It had been a long time since I'd found myself in a serious discussion about the Constitution — and for me these discussions were more firmly grounded in reality than they had ever been in a classroom. For the first time I found myself intently reviewing constitutional issues, not as a student or teacher, but as a parent. It was a critical perspective because it forced me to consider the Constitution in terms of consequences: What kind of guarantees does this document make to my child?

This perspective fueled my outrage at the way warring ideological camps had dominated the debate in recent years over the direction of the country. My view was that both the right and left had adopted take-no-prisoners tactics, and the hardening of their positions had led to a breakdown in respect and acceptance for the validity of opposing views. Like animals marking off their territory in the woods for themselves by urinating around it, I felt that both conservatives and liberals had taken over key issues for their own selfish uses. Conservatives had marked off the right to bear arms, the principle of judicial restraint, "family values," and so forth; liberals had marked off freedom of expression, congressional review, and the idea of a "compassionate government." Each side discounted the barest thread of legitimacy in the other's position for fear of weakening its own. As a father trying to raise children in this increasingly confrontational atmosphere, my frustration evolved into anger at the endless series of false and debilitating choices it has engendered.

As our discussions progressed, then, Gillian found herself face to face with the Mad Moderate. My view of the debate outside was that it could be defined in terms of the First and Second amendments to the Constitution, the First being the amendment of choice for the left, the Second that of the right. Those with a more chaotic world view — where people speak their own minds, write their own thing, go their own way and worship (or not) their own God — lean toward the First Amendment. Those with a more ordered world view who are not entirely confident that others, especially government, will maintain that order, lean toward the Second Amendment.

Although I believe that one of the great luxuries of youth is to feel passionately about things — and nothing short of love itself inspires passion like a flame-forged political ideal — I deliberately aimed to dampen Gillian's political passions with demands for that most moderating of exercises, reflection.

One Monday morning we watched a videotape of the previous night's *60 Minutes* segment that dealt with the proliferation of guns among American schoolchildren. I should have known how my own daughter felt about that, but I didn't. Gillian seemed nonviolent on the surface, but I had no idea how desensitizing the barrage of media violence had been on her psyche. I didn't know if her libertarian posture on rap lyrics extended to guns: if you don't like it, don't buy, don't load, don't shoot, etc. And it was by no means an abstract issue. Tales of guns showing up at teenage parties had already filtered back to us, and in neighboring towns, apparently safe from the violence of downtown L.A., guns were beginning to take a frightening toll on the lives of kids. So I let out a gratified sigh when I heard Gillian audibly gasp at the report of an elementary school teacher who had to disarm a seven-year-old who had brought a loaded gun to class one day.

Nonetheless, we would not ignore Alistair Cooke's essay on America's love affair with the gun. It had always been, he explained, the great equalizer — the way the early settlers evened the sides against the vast, savage, unknown territory they sought to tame; the colonists evened the sides against a larger, more experienced imperial army they sought to expel; the ranch and farm families of the Wild West evened the sides against the rustlers, bandits, and desperados they sought to bring under the rule of law.

It was a lesson free of cant on why the Second Amendment was so important to the framers of the Constitution. In a home such as ours, where guns are neither owned nor honored, it could easily have been a lesson omitted or taught in the politically correct fashion of the day, with a great deal of rhetoric about the gun as the white man's primary instrument of oppression. But both my political and educational philosophies dictated that I not shroud Gillian's intellect in ignorance or propaganda. For better and worse, the gun had played a significant role in shaping the American character and continent, and I wanted her to understand that.

Gillian's libertarian leanings led her to side with the American Civil Liberties Union in opposing the city of L.A.'s ban on gangs' gathering in city parks. This was a freedom of assembly issue, she argued in a paper I asked her to write. I passed up the opportunity to reinforce that enlightened view, asking her to consider the feelings of the residents of the neighborhoods near these parks, who had paid for the parks with their taxes and now could not use them. I was encouraged by Gillian's consideration of that argument, but as she revealed in a subsequent paper, she was not persuaded by it. Persuasion, of course, hadn't been the goal. The goal had been to make her see the complexity and relevance to her life of the freedom of assembly issue and, further, to make her deal with the issue of gangs intellectually, to consider them in a historical and constitutional context.

In seventh grade, she'd dealt with the subject differently.

She'd demonstrated a passing fascination with gangs, sending a real shudder down my spine by occasionally assuming gang walk, dress, and attitude on her way out the door. It was all pretend, of course; her world was far too insulated from the real thing for her to learn any of that lifestyle at first hand. It was also quite natural, according to my recollections of college anthropology and adolescent psychology. Adolescents crave group identity, whether it be the code and colors of a cheerleading squad or a street gang, such identification is critical to their development. Gillian was not a cheerleader, so she was taking her group identity where she found it.

For someone who perceived the home school, subconsciously at least, as a sort of escape from the cruel world, I could have done a better job to keep the demons at bay. I could have filled Gillian's days with music from Mozart, passages from Shelley and Keats, day trips to the Norton Simon and J. Paul Getty museums, and nights gazing at the heavens through a telescope. Certainly there was enough wonder and beauty still extant in the world to occupy our time and energies for nine months while Gillian got a breather from the harsher realities and some kind of appreciation for the finer things. But my instincts as a teacher stood up to my fears as a father, and we pressed on with the business of learning, wherever it would lead us.

One Thursday afternoon in late September it led us to *Boyz N the Hood.* Gillian had been campaigning for us to take in the film as part of a class field trip. I finally overcame my fear of being shot in a theater lobby, as headlines about the film had suggested might happen, and overcame my even greater fear of listening to a soundtrack heavily laden with rap — a musical form that can almost arouse in someone as civilized as myself an uncontrollable urge to open fire on the folks standing in line for popcorn. As it turned out, Gillian and I had one of L.A.'s finest theaters all to ourselves for a matinee, and we settled in for an experience that was considerably different from my own childhood ventures to movies with my father. There we were, father and daughter from the white suburbs, while 20-foot-tall, young black men on the screen in front of us talked dirt about whores, bitches, motherfuckers, and pussy. It was not unfamiliar language to me, nor was it, sadly, unfamiliar to Gillian. Our mutual discomfort was palpable at first, despite our separate, but equal acquaintance with it. Although I can't imagine a film with such language when I was growing up in the fifties, I can imagine my father taking me by the hand and leading me away from one. But such are the times we live in — such is the accepted openness of our society and my commitment as a parent to raise children who use ideas and language judiciously while not shrinking from the ideas and language of others — that I made no such gesture to Gillian. We stayed and watched *Boyz N the Hood* — and were rewarded. The film impressed me as an affirmation of strong, active parenting, especially fathering. The hero who saves the life of Trey, a black youth trying to grow up amid the dangers and degradations of modern urban America is Furious Styles, the boy's father, armed only with a sense of right and wrong. Furious, like Otto Frank before him, essentially announces to the world: *I have taken responsibility for my child, no matter how awesome the task may be. I accept ultimate responsibility for loving, protecting, and making my child better than the world he was born into.*

At the outset of our home schooling, I had projected myself as a teacher who was going to get Gillian to take stock of the world and maybe start spelling correctly, writing in complete sentences, and doing her math on time. I didn't dare anticipate how quickly or profoundly it would affect our personal relationship. Soon after we started, I began noticing that Gillian no longer seemed to be in a hurry to slink through a room that I was in, she used "Dad" as a form of address in her speech more frequently, and she initiated discussions. One day she said, "Do you want me to tell you something surprising?"

I laughed.

She asked, "What's so funny?"

I said, "Most of what you tell me surprises me."

She said, "Tell me about it. That's because I don't have my friends to talk to anymore; I end up telling you everything."

Well, not everything maybe, but our communication had reached levels of openness and understanding that I would not have imagined, at least not while Gillian was in the throes of adolescence — and not while I was in the throes of being the father of an adolescent. As a consequence, our early lessons fairly purred along with warmth and good humor.

One weekend I paid more attention to a fierce Notre Dame–Tennessee football game than to the questions she had prepared on the northern forest segment of *The Living Planet*. On Monday she nailed me for it. She asked me how the sawfly caterpillar defends itself. I didn't know. She couldn't believe I didn't know. She thought I knew everything that didn't concern the life of teenage girls. But I'd tuned into that football game and missed the part about the defensive technique of the sawfly caterpillar.

"Chemical warfare," she informed me. "They make a gum out of resin and put it on the antenna of a scout ant so he can't find his way home.

"What do the bears of the northern forest eat?" she continued, clearly relishing the feel of the upper hand.

I didn't remember anything in the video about the eating

habits of bears, and she could tell, too. Mimicking me, she suggested I use common sense to come up with the answer.

"Berries," I said.

"And what else?"

"Fish," I replied.

"What kind of fish?"

"Trout."

"And what do these trout eat?"

What do the trout eat? How much of that damned game had I watched? I was beginning to feel like a gummed-up little scout ant myself.

"Okay," said she, the taskmaster, softening a bit. "What's the first sign of spring in the northern forest?"

"Crocuses," I guessed.

"Crocuses?" she repeated archly.

"Croci?" I guessed again, squirming like a delinquent twelve-year-old.

"Very good," she announced with a wicked smile, handing me her question paper. I looked at it. There was nothing there about any of this stuff. It'd been sheer improvisation on her part, and she was delighted with her con. So was I.

Another time she protested against my insistence that we read aloud together each morning, usually from the newspaper. She didn't understand why I just didn't read the articles myself since I could read them so much faster than she. I tried to explain my rationale with a story from my freshman year of college. There had been a blonde who had attracted me even though she was always hidden behind a book. I approached her in the cafeteria one day and tried to spark a conversation off the book she was reading. "So tell me about Goethe," I said, pronouncing his name "goeth," as in *Pride goeth before the fall.*

"Well, first off," she replied sharply, cutting me off cleanly at the knees, "he's not Go-eth; he's *Ge(r)*-te. Johannes Wolfgang *Ge(r)*-te."

"I was so humiliated," I told Gillian, "I never got around to asking her out, and it's all because we never practiced pronouncing things correctly around our house when I was growing up."

"Don't worry about it, Dad," she told me. "The guy who looks like the guy I'm going to marry won't even know who Goethe is."

Ka-boom.

Before the home schooling experience, I probably would have overlooked Anita Hill's father when Hill first appeared before the Senate Judiciary Committee hearings regarding Clarence Thomas's nomination to the Supreme Court. But this wisp of an aging black man seated behind his daughter served as mute testimony to the limits of what any father — Otto Frank, Furious Styles, Dan Riley — can do for a child. Mr. Hill's support of his daughter was confined to their private moments. In the public arena, she was on her own, and he could do nothing about it no matter how nasty things got.

Before Hill's appearance, the hearings had simply seemed to illustrate the checks and balances we had seen explained in *America*. We watched and discussed the video, then snapped on the TV, and there it was. History couldn't get any more living than that. But then the talk turned to pubic hairs in the Coke can and Long Dong Silver, and it was hard to imagine the Founding Fathers smiling down upon the proceedings and proudly observing, "There, that's just what we had in mind."

By that point, to be sure, Gillian and I were veterans at listening to raw language together — although this unpleasantness was of an entirely different order. This was the public humiliation of two — politics completely aside — relatively decent human beings and the thoroughgoing mockery of, not one, not two, but all three branches of the U.S. government. It was lamentable civics, of course, but irresistible television, and there was no need to assign it to Gillian. Like much of the nation, she was glued to it throughout. She even called me at work in the afternoons to give me updates on the proceedings, expressing an enthusiasm about politics and government I'd never anticipated.

Maybe it wasn't such bad civics after all. When it was over, Gillian let it be known that she wanted to be president someday. I was amazed, first, because Gillian had always been so reticent about any ambitions at all (beyond owning a horse). Second, because I believed that wanting to grow up to be president was far too quaint a notion for any kid nowadays. Third, because I was convinced that my own cynicism about American politics surely must have infected both my children. Finally, I truly couldn't believe that anyone watching the spectacle of those hearings would ever want to have anything whatsoever to do with public office. She didn't say why she wanted to be president; I guessed that the idea of a woman president standing up to all those middle-age white guys running the show appealed to her audaciousness. If nothing else had been learned during those hearings, one thing was certain: it would take an audacious woman to accomplish such a feat.

Occasionally, I amused myself by speculating about Gillian's becoming president: What character flaws would she have to overcome? Which of her strengths would best serve her and the country? What obstacles would still remain to her sex? Would I sleep more soundly at night knowing Gillian was in the White House given that she had caused me so much sleeplessness in my own house?

And what about those childhood transgressions of hers? In light of, or more appropriately, in the shadow of the Thomas hearings, for what past sins would Gillian be made to answer? How far back would the record go on her? Would some rabid journalist in dogged pursuit of the public's right to know torpedo her candidacy with the revelation that when she was thirteen years old she wrote a letter to her parents telling them she was going out for a walk and went to the teen center dance instead?

The question, as it turned out, was not an idle one. About two months into our home schooling, Gillian started to fall behind in her journal. When I called her on it, she said she was running out of things to say. "All I ever write about are horses," she said, "and I'm even beginning to bore myself on the subject." It was an extraordinary admission, since Gillian can talk enough about horses to make Mr. Ed's eyes glaze over.

I reminded her that Anne Frank didn't have trouble coming up with things to write about, and she was stuck in that tiny apartment with the same people day and night for years. To which Gillian replied rather fiercely, "But that's because she didn't know the whole world was going to be reading it. I'd shoot somebody if they ever printed stuff I'd written like that."*

A week earlier we had been reading Anne Frank's thoughts about the possibility of her diary's being published. When I pointed out how ironic her comments were, since her diary turned out to be the most famous book ever written by a

---

*Gillian has given her full consent for my use of her journal, letters, and other papers in this book.

teenager, Gillian totally surprised me by saying, "I'm going to change that." It was another uncharacteristic expression of ambition on her part. First the presidency, then a book. I suddenly had Superchild on my hands! But within a week she'd had a change of heart, which dismayed and bewildered me. I asked about her boast to write a great book. She said she had only been joking and that I take her too seriously. "When I say I want to write a screenplay," she complained, "you start giving me lessons in screenplay writing. When I say I want to learn Italian, you start giving me Italian lessons. I want to do this stuff, but not now. You're pushing me too fast."

Was it just a passing mood or were these cracks I was beginning to see in the hallowed halls of the Dan Riley School for a Girl? Indeed, some discouraging fissures were definitely beginning to open around our little utopian schoolworks.

For one, although I felt my own relationship with Gillian had greatly improved, the same could not be said for her relations with Lorna and Meagan. Returning from a business trip six weeks into the home schooling, Lorna unloaded on me about Gillian and how their relationship had deteriorated. No particular incident had set her off. It was an emotional buildup stemming, she declared, from my shutting her out of the home school. As a result, she said, Gillian had begun to treat her "like dirt." Lorna then ran off an impressive list of unflattering adjectives to describe Gillian's behavior of late: angry, abusive, mean, and insulting topped the list.

It was not that their relationship hadn't had its own low moments in the past. What was depressing was the implication of the home school in creating a new low. I'd had an inkling of such troubles stirring in the background, but I'd focused on the schooling in the belief that its blossoming would soon be in the foreground of all our lives. The night of the blowup, I went so far as to suggest to Lorna that what she was going through with Gillian at the moment was precisely because the home schooling was working so well: Gillian was identifying so strongly with Anne Frank, whose relationship with her mother was going through a very tough stage.

"Mummy's natures are completely strange to me," Anne wrote in one entry. "I can understand my own friends better than my own mother." Gillian wrote in her own journal, "My mom is trying to be like Anne's mom, and I am feeling like Anne herself."

This analysis helped move the situation out of the emotional realm and into the intellectual for the time being. Although still not happy to serve as Gillian's cathartic punching bag or to stand on the outside looking in at the home school, Lorna decided to read Anne Frank's diary for herself to see what insights she could gather and what might lie ahead while we rode out what we hoped would be a passing storm.

The blame for the mounting tension between Meagan and Gillian might also be put at Anne's secret doorstep. Anne and her sister, Margot, were involved in some intense sibling rivalry — over attentions from their father, over relationships with their mother, over the affections of the young boy who shared their hideout. But kids don't need to learn about sibling rivalry from a book.

Meagan had been an indifferent student herself through most of school, but in her senior year of high school she became very serious about academics, even more so once she got to college. With the energy and enthusiasm of the best of college freshmen, she suddenly wanted to know all about everything — and she wanted my help in learning it. She was living at home, so we spent hours together in the sheer pursuit of knowledge. It was a truly wondrous time, but the home schooling effectively brought an end to it. Meagan, now serious about life and learning, openly expressed her resentment about the home school. She claimed, half in jest — but only half — that the opportunity was being wasted on Gillian and wondered aloud and often how come no one came up with such a great idea when she was a struggling student. From Gillian's viewpoint, Meagan was becoming more and more like Margot, with her cutting comments and superior attitude, "only Margot's smarter and Meagan tries harder to be more annoying."

One morning I broke my own prohibition against bringing family matters into school discussions. Anne had written in her diary about her own two natures, so I asked Gillian if she thought everyone had two natures. She thought they did. I asked her if she could analyze Meagan's two natures. She said, "Sometimes she's very sweet, and sometimes she's very mean." To illustrate the latter part, she told me a story about Meagan borrowing some shoes of hers. Gillian had said that she could as long as she herself wasn't going to be wearing them. Assuming that meant Gillian wasn't going to be wearing them, Meagan borrowed them. But then Gillian got a call to join a friend at the mall, which meant she would be wearing them and Meagan couldn't borrow them. But Meagan already had them on and an entire outfit to match and wasn't about to take them off. A battle royal ensued, with Meagan's taking off the shoes, throwing them into Gillian's room, and vowing never to borrow anything from Gillian again as long as she lived. Gillian then took the shoes and threw them back into Meagan's room, insisting that Meagan wear them. Meagan quickly put them on and was out the door.

"She always does that to me," said Gillian. "She always makes me feel bad, so I give in."

I then told Gillian about Solomon offering to slice the baby in half to settle a dispute over its parentage. "If you had come to me with the problem, I would have handled it like Solomon," I said. "I would've given a shoe to each of you."

"That wouldn't have worked," she countered. "Then neither of us would've worn them."

"The point is that one of you would've had to rise above the petty squabbling. One of you would've had to call upon a generosity of spirit to save you from both being so unhappy." I sighed and considered a thought that had crossed my mind now and then in twenty-one years of fatherhood, then added, "I sometimes worry that we don't have enough religion around here."

"What we don't have enough of is clothes," Gillian said.

The wisdom of Solomon, the patience of Job, the resourcefulness of Merlin . . . what was becoming increasingly clear was that I was going to need all of that and more to get through the weeks ahead with the home schooling project still intact.

In November, Gillian's former classmates started work on their junior high yearbook. In the early weeks of our school she had been going back to the junior high to eat lunch with her friends, but that ended when the administration found out she was no longer a student there. Now the phone, which had been her vital link to the world of her friends, isolated her even more as the news that crackled along the line was all about who was being nominated for best looking, class clown, best hair, and so forth — trivial, meaningless stuff to a forty-year-old, the essence of life to a thirteen-year-old.

The sense of growing estrangement from friends and normal junior high life was becoming evident. Gillian was incrementally taking more time before appearing at the kitchen counter for the beginning of classes each morning, thereby demonstrating that, yes, it was possible to be late for home school. One morning she appeared late, wrapped in a blanket, with a look on her face that dared me to even say good morning. She dropped her head into her folded arms on the counter, knocking off a pile of the day's books and videos. I said nothing, waiting for her to pick them up. After a long but silent wait she did, at which point I rearranged our schedule for the day and led her to the VCR; another benefit to using video was the escape it provided from such moments.

On November 17, Gillian wrote in her journal:

You can be my teacher and my dad without doing anything, but being my friend takes a little extra effort. I guess you think it's not important though cuz you're already playing two major roles in my life. I don't think you can handle three. I have a good teacher and a bad dad. I would rather it be the other way around, so I want to go back to Redwood so you can practice being a real dad instead of trying so hard to be a teacher.

A few days later she wrote:

I wanted this to work. I really did, but it's not, and you can't deny it. It's painful 4 you and me.

I thought we would make it all the way through, but here it is only November, and I'm feeling more pain now than ever.

There's no reason 4 me to write every day because my feelings haven't changed from the 17th.

I would rather go to school and have my real dad back than have a teacher I can hardly bear and a dad who knows nothing but pain from me.

The next weekend, she and a friend, J, left for a sleepover at H's house. When I called H's the next morning, H's mom told me there had been no sleepover that night. When I called J's mom, I was told that she understood the sleepover was to be at our house.

We had come to a crisis. From the beginning of the school year I had tried to avoid having parental discipline interfere with teaching, since I knew the home school depended upon Gillian's voluntary cooperation. I had no grades to hold over her head, no vice principal or guidance counselor to refer her to when things got rough. I had to do it myself, and I knew that if teaching priorities were overwhelmed by discipline priorities, learning would cease, and it would be time to pack the whole thing in. This situation was the severest test yet to the home schooling; there could be no avoiding it. There had been a major transgression that called for major disciplining, and it was going to be impossible to stop it from poisoning the school day. We grounded Gillian from sleepovers indefinitely (privately, I vowed it would be until she was eighteen).

The following Monday morning was the coldest day in California history, figuratively if not literally. I was not sure of how to handle the aftermath of the punishment. Gillian's disposition was icy if not hostile. Opening the morning paper and discussing the future of the Baltic states did not seem in order, so I suggested we begin with a walk down to KC's corral. She silently acquiesced.

On the way, I drummed up some uncharacteristic interest in the horse and tossed out a few questions. She offered faint, monosyllabic answers from three steps ahead of me. When we reached a crossroads to the corral, she turned right toward a shortcut through a very muddy field. I was turning left toward a somewhat longer but drier route. I stopped and urged her in my direction. She stopped but insisted on going her own way. Suddenly we were facing each other as adversaries in the glistening morning sun, both steely eyed for the showdown we knew was upon us. This really wasn't about which way to the ranch; this was about authority. I was embodying it; Gillian was questioning it. The irony of my position as an admirer of that QUESTION AUTHORITY bumper sticker was not lost on me, but this was no time to be enchanted by irony. Too much was at stake, and I think it was only because I knew I had more at stake than she did that I was able to outlast her. She finally relinquished a few steps in my direction. Without waiting for her to surrender all the distance between us, I turned and led the way to the corral. There she fed KC, and on our return home she cut three steps off her pace and politely talked to me about the horse.

During the next three days, however, we were both very tentative with each other. The Dan Riley School for a Girl, it seemed, like the public schools it sought to replace, was suddenly a school at risk.

6

THE SECOND QUARTER

MY DECISION TO END the first quarter at Thanksgiving was completely arbitrary. There was no educational theory behind my plan to divide the year into four quarters of approximately nine weeks each. However, as Gillian and I dragged our beaten spirits toward the break, a vacation never seemed more critical. Even without the crisis of the past few weeks swirling around us, I still would have anticipated this break as eagerly as any since my days as a public school teacher. One of the first lessons I had learned was that preparing a day's worth of classes for one child was as exhausting as doing it for a hundred. And whereas past holidays always seemed to be burdened with research papers to be read and graded, this holiday had its own special burden: the Dan Riley School for a Girl was in serious danger of falling apart.

Gillian was thoroughly despondent, and it was clear that the primary objective of the long weekend was to restore her emotional equilibrium. When Lorna and I called her into the den for a talk on Friday night, she proceeded to pour out a heartful of teenage miseries. She insisted that all her friendships were dying because of the home schooling. She said she got to see her friends only on weekends, and if things went wrong between them, there was no time to make up, no notes to be exchanged during third period, no lunchroom secrets to be revealed, no weekends to be planned. No weekends. Period. More and more, she cried, the weekends went on without her.

She begged to have sleepovers restored, claiming she really did stay at H's the weekend before. "We were supposed to sleep over S's house," she said, "but she came over here after a fight with her mom and didn't want to go home again, and since I already had permission for a sleepover we went to H's, but H's mom didn't know we were there because we came in through her bedroom window and left early in the morning."

It wasn't so much a talk as a primal scream. The renowned Gillian toughness seeped from her body, and she tearfully collapsed before us in a heap in the corner of the room. Lorna and I had seen her bounce off a hundred rocky roads before without even wincing; we knew we were witnessing genuine hurt this time.

I believe the hard-line approach to child rearing has the same appeal that it does to social structuring or global ordering. For those with the power, it's quick, painless, and illusory: the powerful believe that they've solved their problem, enhanced their power, and done what is best for both them and their victims. Sometimes they're right. But what's certain about a one-note song is that it's not really a song, and the same answer applied to a multitude of questions is never the answer.

In what would be the first of many spiritual reference points in the second quarter, I fell back upon some favorite lines from the Book of Ecclesiastes:

For everything there is a season . . .
A time to build up; a time to break down
A time for war; a time for peace.

Gillian's journal entry that night was as follows:

Sorry about the past few entries. I get a little down sometimes. Please let me go to Redwood just for one month.
Please. I'll never ask for anything again, and in February
I'll be back to home school. Please, Dad, this means a lot
to me, including some dying friendships. PLEASE. I'll be
your best friend — seeing how I don't have any now!

We lifted Gillian's sleepover restriction, which didn't seem
to console her much. She said she didn't think she was going
to be invited to many more sleepovers anyway. We suggested
she hold one herself and invite her friends. It seemed a positive
suggestion, but Gillian was beyond all suggestion.

On Monday morning we were in the car, about to head
down to feed KC, when an argument flared up over the choice
of radio station. I'd gotten into the car first, to warm it up, and
turned on the radio just in time to hear a DJ ask his sidekick if
he'd seen the previous night's *60 Minutes?* I had, and one of
the segments had made such an impact on me that I'd ended
up dreaming about it. Called "Camille," it was about a Florida woman who was caring for seventeen mentally disabled
children in her home. Camille came across as so heroic that
when I had a nightmare that very night about being pursued
by giant rats it was she who came to my rescue. Since morning
DJs are such a reliable source of crass, sophomoric humor, my
engines were revved to fly into a fine fury over the wisecrack I
felt sure was coming. Just then Gillian got into the car and
immediately changed the station. I snapped at her to get the
other station back.

"Right after this song," she said.

"Now," I said.

"It's my favorite song," she said.

"Now!" I shouted.

"It's almost over," she said.

I reached down to the dial myself and changed the station back to the first station in time to hear the DJ announce that it was 7:43 and that he'd be back after a break for traffic and weather. Gillian could not believe that I'd cut away from her "favorite" song for this. I was too livid to explain. Thus do great experiments in parenting turn on such incidents. In retrospect, I am overwhelmed by the monumental pettiness of the entire affair. It was pitched pretty much at the level of Meagan and Gillian's shoe war.

Our mutual anger continued unabated through the feeding of the horse and the ride home. By the time we got there, I realized we had to cut through it quickly if any learning was to be accomplished that morning. I told Gillian to write down her version of what had just transpired and I would do the same.

The exercise imposed a badly needed cooling-off period on both of us. When we were done, we asked Lorna to join us and evaluate our respective positions. Having it all down on paper saved us from the usual volleys of "he said" and "she said" that usually serve only to confuse and inflame such circumstances. Lorna did not pass judgment on either of our positions; she simply led us through an analysis of our two papers. The goal was to objectify as much as possible an irrational event and to show Gillian a less contentious way of resolving a conflict.

Gillian seemed a little wary at first. I think the stress of the preceding weeks had left her feeling very vulnerable. I also think she felt at a disadvantage in having her writing measured against mine and having the measurement done by another adult — another parent. But Lorna's evenhanded treatment and the evident strength of Gillian's paper boosted her confidence. She became increasingly animated as the discussion progressed, showing more signs of life than we had seen from her in days. Even I had to admit that Gillian's was the far more objective recounting of events in the car. My own had been severely undermined by my simmering emotions over the anticipated insult to the heroic lady from *60 Minutes*.

The critical outcome of the entire incident, however, was our establishing the writing of "position papers" as a mutually agreeable means for dealing with future conflicts. Neither of us imagined there wouldn't be any further need for such means. In fact, Gillian suggested that we start dealing with all of our controversies in the school setting. She said she found that things built up too much inside when problems developed between us and we put them aside for the sake of the lessons. I didn't know if I was ready to buy into that, but I was glad that Gillian was now contributing ideas about how best to conduct the school.

Coincidentally, the previous day's newspaper had contained an article on home schooling in our town. I saved it for Gillian to read, hopeful that she might feel less isolated by reading about other kids going through the same experience. In response to the article, Gillian, on her own, wrote the following letter to the paper:

Dear L.A. Times,

As I was flipping through the paper, I happened to notice your article on the home studies program that is a growing fad.

I am 13 years old and currently in the program myself with my dad as my teacher.

The program has its good points . . . and its bad points.

First, I don't think parents should do this if they're doing it just to protect their children from gang violence, drugs, peer pressure or growing up. So many people see this as a way to shelter their children from the reality of the craziness going on in our world. People must not forget that children do almost half of their learning on the playground at school. When you take your children out of school, you're taking away most of their social life, which is a big problem and was hidden in your article.

Friends are one of the most important things in a young adult's life. I personally am dependent on my friends for everything. If I lost them, as I came so close to doing as a result of the home studies program, I would feel completely lost with no sense of direction. Parents sometimes forget how important their friends were to them and don't even try to imagine how important they are to us, the younger generation.

Parents, please remember that if your children can read, write, do math, and whatnot, great! But when they're 35 years old, not married, and friends aren't there for support when they just lost their job selling real estate because they don't know how to deal and communicate with people, they won't be very happy. Where are those early playground days when you need them?!

Sincerely,
Jillian Riley

The crisis in her life had definitely sharpened Gillian's perception. The article, unnoticed by me, was heavily slanted toward an adult point of view. Discouraging words were limited to these few by one of the students: "There aren't many kids around," he said, echoing Gillian's sentiments, "and that's kind of depressing, seeing the same people every day."

His words were quickly rebutted by a home schooling mom, however. "I don't feel it's necessary for them to be with large groups of children," she said, echoing my own sentiments. "A lot of the socialization kids get at school is negative socialization."

Writing the letter had a salutary effect on Gillian. When it was done, she launched into a funny, insightful monologue that ranged freely over the subject of adolescence in general and home schooling, friendships, telephoning, and writing notes in particular. It was the most effusive she'd been since I'd asked her why the suicide rate was so high among today's teenagers.

She said she actually liked being taught at home — from an academic standpoint, at least. But she thought I was really missing the significance of the social interaction. I said I thought she was exaggerating her situation; the phone seemed to ring for her now more than ever. She told me I didn't understand those phone calls: "If I call one of my friends and someone is visiting who doesn't like me, they'll cut me off, and then call back later to make it up. Then sometimes they'll only call when they have someone over their house and they're trying to impress them with how many people they know, so they call everybody."

Then, she said, she gets calls like the one she just got from W, who likes to make everyone think she's the only one they can trust. "She called me and said, 'Gillian, I want you to know how much I respect you for putting up with all you have to put up with.' And I asked her what she was talking about, and she tells me, 'Well, everybody's talking about you behind your back all the time. But you don't have to worry about me. I don't.'" Gillian added, "She always does that. She calls you up and tells you when someone's talking behind your back, but while it's happening, she doesn't do anything to stop it. None of them do." I thought it was time to introduce a new vocabulary word to describe the world of her friendships — Byzantine. She put it to use immediately. Whenever subsequent phone calls or visits with friends took a curious turn, she would shake her head and say, "Byzantine."

As a further sign of her recovery, she invited me to her room to see her latest project. She had organized all the notes she had received from friends over the past two years into three-ring binders according to author. Notes from her best friend, B, took up one binder alone. This voluminous collection of dispatches from the frontier of teenagehood gave a lie to the notion that kids don't write anymore.

I suggested that she keep writing her notes, only now she should put them in envelopes, stick a stamp on them, and mail them — just as in the good old days. She suggested I start a journal, too. To her surprise, I told her I was already keeping one. Positive suggestions all around. Things were beginning to look up.

Gillian and I had put in two positive days together, and I was hopeful that we were getting her personal distress in order and were back on the road to learning. But Lorna still had her reservations and aired one over the dinner table. Since the initial discussion about home schooling, when she and Gillian first learned of my plan, Lorna had kept any serious doubts she had between the two of us — and, I assumed, between her and Meagan. Any critical comments voiced in front of Gillian were generally cloaked in humor. Both Lorna and Meagan often took lighthearted jabs at the "so-called school" Gillian and I were conducting out in the morning sun each day, occasionally stretched out on patio furniture and looking none too belabored. During this particular dinner, however, just days removed from our most difficult time with the home school, Lorna was anything but lighthearted. She said that she thought Gillian was watching entirely too much TV during her unsupervised afternoons and that whenever she, Lorna, questioned her on it, Gillian would snap at her. Then, as if on cue, Gillian snapped. "You're not my teacher," she declared in a loud and obnoxious manner. "You don't know how much work I do or when I do it. You just walk in and start yelling at me all the time."

Lorna dropped all pretense at motherly patience and understanding. She got up from the table and fiercely announced, "I'm not going to sit here and take this." Then she marched off down the hall to her office.

Gillian stormed off to her room.

I was left alone at the dinner table, feeling as if my puzzle had just been kicked over after I'd gotten 490 of my 500 pieces in place. For the next half hour I conducted a kind of down-home version of Mideast shuttle diplomacy. First, I was in Gillian's room, reminding her that regardless of her role in the school, Lorna was still a legitimate authority figure in Gillian's life and that if she had questions about the direction of Gillian's afternoons, she was entitled to answers without attitude. Then I was in Lorna's office, just the way countless teachers, defending their competence, face angry parents every day, explaining that I was dutifully leaving Gillian with what I thought were two hours of work each afternoon and that each morning she was being responsive to those assignments. I didn't think I could complain if she was finishing early and turning on TV.

After I'd said all I could say on the matter, I escaped to the public library, seeking refuge from what had been for me an emotionally exhausting four days. I hoped that in my absence, mother and daughter would come together and work out the problem on their own. When I returned, however, the signs were ominous. I passed by Gillian's room and found it empty. I then found Lorna working at her desk under the assumption that Gillian was in her room. There had been no contact between them. Lorna had opted to wait for an apology. But it was now after nine on a chilly weeknight, and it was clear that we were going to have to wait for more than an apology. There were no signs of Gillian in or around the house. And unlike her memorable venture to the teen center dance, which more or less launched this phase of our lives, this time there was nothing left behind in her room — no light, no music, no note.

There was, however, this entry in her journal.

> Damn — isn't there 1 time in my life that everyone will be happy with me just for a few minutes.
>
> It seems as though I am always in disagreement with one of you. We used to fight a lot, but there were times I got along with both of you. Just this morning I was thinking about what a great mom I have, and now . . . well, I'm thinking far from that.
>
> Can't you see? Just this one time, hold it in. I'm having a bit of a problem trying to get everything even. I'm going through HELL right now. Can't 1 person be there 4 me?!!!

I drove around the neighborhood looking for her while Lorna called her friends. The obvious question is why didn't we dial 911. Partially because we knew Gillian had initiated this incident herself and was not likely to be a victim, partially because we derived comfort from some cold FBI statistics that named our city the safest in America, and partially because we'd been through this before when Gillian and her best friend, B, had disappeared until three in the morning. I wasn't happy about having the police involved at that time and wasn't about to call them this time. It was pride, pure and simple. This was a family matter, and family matters get handled in a family way.

By 11 P.M. Lorna and I had resumed the roles we had played in these nocturnal dramas since Meagan's birth: Lorna went to sleep, confident that all would be right in the morning; I worked myself into a full panic. My color catalogue of nightmares was open before me. Gillian had simply gone out for a walk around the block, I determined, but a predator, a statistical aberration in Thousand Oaks, had seen her and abducted her. Or she had decided that our conflicts were irreconcilable and had decided to run off and join the growing legions of teenage street people. Or she had decided to teach us a lesson once and for all, to indulge in the ultimate teenage fantasy — an early, self-inflicted death.

I paced the house, the streets, and my well-worn, discomfiting imagination until dawn. Everything came in for questioning — the home school, the home itself; too much discipline, too little discipline; not enough love, too much understanding; the move from New England, the move to California; the media, the church, the atom bomb, rock 'n' roll. Some people can blame all these problems on rock 'n' roll. Sometimes I envy them.

I reflected on a night years earlier when Meagan was sixteen and put me through a similar experience. I'd found a boy in her room at one in the morning. When he'd heard me approach her room, he'd fallen to the floor, flat on his stomach, and tried desperately to burrow through the concrete slab. I escorted him to the front door and bade him farewell

with as much icy contempt as I could generate. I wasn't at all
sure how to deal with Meagan. She, being the elder and
generally more responsible one, had given us few opportuni-
ties to discipline her. As I passed her door, I stuck my head in
and said that we would talk about the matter in the morning.
But when I got to bed, I couldn't sleep. I tossed and turned,
trying to decide what I was going to say to her in that morning
talk.

So I went back to her room to wake her up and improvise
the conversation right there in the still of the night. When I got
to her room, however, she was gone. It was two or three in the
morning by then, but I stormed out the front door to find her;
mercifully, I caught a shadowy glimpse of her almost immediately, making her way back toward the house. I beat a hasty
retreat to her room and waited. As she came through the
sliding glass door, I hit her with a blunt question: "What in the
hell is going on?" She gave me a look that said, That's a good
question. She told me she'd been wrestling with it herself
lately. She wasn't quite sure, but she said she'd recently been
overwhelmed by a tremendous need to unburden herself of
the tiresome image of quiet, boring, reliable Meagan Day
Riley.

That night, in keeping with an obvious behavior pattern of
my own, I reached for a book — *Demian* by Hermann Hesse,
another standard from my teaching repertoire. I turned to
a passage which, I recalled, remarkably echoed Meagan's
speech that evening. It comes after the book's young hero,
guilty of eating fruit from a forbidden tree, has been black-
mailed by the neighborhood bully into stealing from his parents. He is confronted by his father, who knows nothing of the
theft but is angry at him for tracking mud into the house. I
read it aloud for both of us:

"I knew I now had a secret, a sin which I would have to expiate alone. Perhaps I stood at a parting of the ways, perhaps I would now belong among the wicked forever, share their secrets, depend on them, obey them, have to become their kind. I had acted the man and hero and now had to bear the consequences.

". . . I felt superior to my father! Momentarily, I felt a certain loathing for his ignorance. His upbraiding me for muddy boots seemed pitiful. 'If you only knew' crossed my mind as I stood there like a criminal being cross-examined for a stolen loaf of bread when the actual crime was murder. It was an odious, hostile feeling, but it was strong and deeply attractive, and shackled me more than anything else to my secret and my guilt . . .

"[This moment] was the first rent in the holy image of my father, it was the first fissure in the columns that had upheld my childhood, which every individual must destroy before he can become himself. The inner, the essential line of our fate consists of such invisible experiences. Such fissures and rents grow together again, heal and are forgotten, but in the most secret recesses they continue to live and bleed.

"I immediately felt such dread at this new feeling that I could have fallen down before my father and kissed his feet to ask forgiveness. But one cannot apologize for something fundamental, and a child knows and feels this as well and as deeply as any sage."

I read the passage again while desperately waiting for Gillian to appear out of the night. For years I'd taught it from the safe vantage point of educator. But with Meagan and now with Gillian, I found myself reappraising it as a parent and facing its full consequences. "There is no breakthrough without breakage," wrote Norman O. Brown in *Love's Body*, another favorite of mine. I'd understood that rather clearly as a teacher who offered a sympathetic ear to hundreds of adolescents struggling to break with their own parents. But the parent, unlike the teacher, doesn't get to turn the child out at three in the afternoon, doesn't have the luxury of creating a distance from any particular child, doesn't have the option of treating the often painful process of identity formation as mere academic exercise. The child is the creation of the parent, who inevitably feels the break as acutely as the child does. Often it's confusing, hurtful, and scary. Surely it was the night Gillian disappeared.

I dozed in and out of late-night TV; then, around 6 A.M., I got back into the car and searched the neighborhood again. I found her down at the barn with KC, raking up the corral. Unseen, I watched her. She was safe. The critical question had been answered, so I decided to leave the others until later. I was too tired.

While I tried to recover the night's sleep, Lorna took Gillian out for breakfast, and they had a reconciliation. They apologized for blowing up at each other over the dinner table. Gillian promised to be more responsive when asked about her work. Lorna promised to ask in a less nagging fashion. They planned a communications class together for the home school.

"She spent the night in the barn," Lorna told me. "She said she felt like Huckleberry Finn when he was floating down the river without any troubles. She said she wanted to live like that next summer."

If Anne Frank had been the spirit of the first quarter, Huck Finn was definitely the spirit of the second. Having been burned twice now by the literature studies at the Dan Riley

School for a Girl, Lorna expressed considerable wariness at what reading I had in store for Gillian in the third quarter. "Not *Rosemary's Baby,* I hope," she said in a rare display of dark humor.

Although *The Adventures of Huckleberry Finn* had been a staple of every novel course I'd ever taught in public school, I was hesitant about introducing it to Gillian at the beginning of the second quarter. I was concerned that she might not be ready for it, and if she weren't, I might ruin it for her forever. I don't think this is an uncommon dilemma for either educators or parents. If we force feed our kids something we think will be good for them, they may gag and never acquire a taste for it; yet if we don't expose them to certain "classic" things when they're young, they may never experience them.

Although I had a personal and professional track record of success with *Huckleberry Finn,* Gillian, at thirteen was three to four years younger than the students to whom I'd taught it before, and if I failed and made her an enemy of Huck Finn, that alone, in my mind, would be grounds for closing our school.

I asked Meagan for advice. She'd gotten her introduction to Huck in public school, with negligible results. She encouraged me to teach it to Gillian. "You're her best chance for liking it," she told me. "She's sure not going to find anybody in high school who cares about it as much as you do."

My caring for Huck extended beyond the literary merits of his story. I often worry about the very survival of the boy himself. Mark Twain's book has been under almost constant attack since its publication: the right attacks for its satirizing of religion and social conventions; the left, for its portrayal of blacks and women; perhaps a rear-guard action from mirthless Shakespearean zealots, for its lampooning of the Bard.

The brazenness with which the self-righteous loot and riot in the marketplace of ideas is an unpleasant sight.

This isn't to say that Huck is not a threatening figure, however. His story may be the most subversive teenage story ever told. He indulges in that most romantic teenage fantasy — he stages his own death and watches his friends mourn him; he outwits an abusive father; he wriggles free of a restrictive society; he struggles with sexual identity; most of all, he lies. The crimes, bigotries, hypocrisies, and deceits of the adult world around him are so pervasive that he can survive them only by lying. He lies from necessity and from the heart, but lies nonetheless.

The problem with presenting Huck as a hero so passionately is that you end up endorsing his actions. I knew that, in introducing my thirteen-year-old daughter to him, there was a risk she'd be seduced by him and try to follow in his footsteps . . . and so she had.

Could she similarly be seduced by Jesus? Unlike many home schools, ours was not designed to promote a particular religious creed. Even in my own school, I was going to toe the First Amendment line on that issue. But it was not easy.

In growing up Catholic, the comfort of knowing Jesus was second only to the unconscious comfort of the womb itself. As I grew older, however, even as I attended a seminary, earning a master's degree in religion, my relationship with Jesus evolved, becoming, in time, almost entirely abstract — a sometimes stimulating but soulless effort to fix Jesus there among the archetypes. It wasn't until I made a nostalgic trip to the Santa Barbara Mission on the Easter before the home school began that I came to an important realization about Jesus and myself as a child: he was less important to me as a divinity than as a model of goodness. The further revelation I had was that in depriving my own children of the spiritual Jesus, I had deprived them of a model of goodness that had been so essential to my own development. I'd left in his place only myself or various cultural icons — the Madonnas and Michael Jacksons — all of us too human for the job. I realized too late how valuable a model of virtue is to young children trying to grow up in a world filled with so much decadence, cynicism, and despair.

In finally deciding to introduce some "religious" teaching into the Dan Riley School for a Girl, I was also moved by a practical consideration. I doubted that a child who had been raised in a religiously neutral environment, as Gillian had been, could fully appreciate art that used religion as a reference point. I recalled my frustration in trying to teach *One Flew over the Cuckoo's Nest* many years earlier. Ken Kesey's classic is rich in Christian imagery, but it was difficult to get students with a weak grasp of those images to appreciate his use of them or the full dimensions of the novel. I didn't want Gillian to be in that position. If she went through life without knowing the frame of reference for those symbols, I believed, she would be as disadvantaged mythically in our culture as her not knowing the times tables would disadvantage her mathematically. Further, I doubted that she could truly experience the sense of rage provoked by Twain at an ideal betrayed, such as when Huck Finn goes against the Christian teaching of his society to help steal Jim out of slavery. "All right then, I'll *go* to hell," Huck declares, giving in to what he'd been taught was his own "wickedness," thus turning Christianity on its head.

Could Gillian, who might not recognize Christianity standing upright, ever hope to recognize it on its head?

I could not roll back the clock — or the stone, as it were — on this. Gillian's spiritual life was hers to make of it what she would. But if our school was going to be bold enough to seek out lessons in *Boyz N the Hood,* it could be bold enough to seek out lessons in *Jesus of Nazareth.*

Gillian and I watched the movie together. She was fascinated by the symbolism of the virgin birth, the walk on water, the temptation in the desert, the Judas kiss, the doubting Thomas, the crucifixion and the resurrection. The intent of the lesson, of course, was to prepare her for the poetry of T. S. Eliot, the films of Fellini, the paintings of Michelangelo, and all the other great art that relies on Christian symbolism. As irony would have it, however, the first application she made was in detecting the use of Christian symbolism in the performance and persona of one of her own heroes, Madonna.

Beyond promoting an academic understanding of Christianity, I wanted Gillian to have at least a feel for what I always believed to be the essential message of Christ's life — the power of forgiveness. So whenever that message was expressed in our other studies, I was sure to draw the connection. I often pointed out that as much as Mark Twain, through Huck, exposed the hypocrisy of Christian society, Huck himself was almost the perfect embodiment of genuine Christian virtue. Through his adventures he constantly demonstrates tolerance, charity, and above all forgiveness for just about everyone he meets, even the conniving king and duke, who had made his and Jim's life so wretched. Upon learning of their awful fate, he reflects: "I see they had the king and duke astraddle a rail — that is, I knowed it was the king and duke, though they was all over tar and feathers, and didn't look like nothing in the world that was human . . . Well, it made me sick to see it; and I was sorry for them poor pitiful rascals, it seemed like I couldn't ever feel any hardness against them any more in the world."

There were lessons, too, in the morning paper. One day it carried a statement by the former Mideast hostage Terry Anderson. After his five-year ordeal, he was asked how he felt about his Arab captors. "I don't hate anybody," he said. "I'm a Christian and a Catholic, and I really believe that. And it's required of me that I forgive, no matter how hard that may be. And I'm determined to do that." I asked Gillian to focus on three words in Anderson's statement — "required," "hard," and "determined" — in order to underscore the challenge of Christ's teaching.

Not long after, we had occasion to take the lesson beyond Madonna's music videos. Gillian had already given up on the idea of going through the entire year without any breaks when I came to her door early one December morning to find the following note:

NOBODY WAKE ME.
I HAVE THE DAY OFF!

I was livid. The night before, we had discussed the prospect of this day off to coincide with a public school day off, and I'd said that if we had a good half-day lesson, I'd consider giving her the other half off. So not only was her note bossy, rude, and impersonal, but it also flew in the face of my clearly stated position. I stood outside her door, briefly contemplating numerous unpleasant ways to wake her. Had my anger not been so unbridled, I believe I would have gone for the bucket of ice water over the head, but I simply burst through her door and bellowed, "Get up! Now!" Then I left, slamming the door behind me.

I believe she grasped the full extent of my anger and was

beginning to grasp the spiritual message we'd been discussing in recent weeks as well. On the way down to feed the horse that morning, she introduced me to a Don Henley song, "Heart of the Matter." She turned up the volume and hit the repeat button so I'd be sure to hear the lyrics above the deafening silence between us:

> These times are so uncertain
> There's a yearning undefined
> . . . people filled with rage
> We all need a little tenderness
> How can love survive in such a graceless age?
> The trust and self-assurance that lead to happiness
> They're the very things we kill, I guess
> Pride and competition
> cannot fill these empty arms
> And the work I put between us
> doesn't keep me warm . . .
> I've been trying to get down
> to the heart of the matter
> Because the flesh will get weak
> and the ashes will scatter
> So I'm thinking about forgiveness
> Forgiveness. . . .

In the months that followed, "Heart of the Matter" virtually become our school song. It almost served as a mantra for us, we played it so often — especially during difficult times. Unfortunately, there was no shortage of those.

Lorna and Gillian had another major blowup, the causes of which can't bear too much analysis without bogging down in muddy little details. Suffice it to say that Lorna was properly angry at Gillian for a typically teenage act of negligence and gave her a punishment. Gillian matter-of-factly accepted the punishment, simultaneously asking Lorna to drive her to a friend's house. Lorna was incredulous. Her original anger was now compounded by hurt that Gillian was exhibiting no remorse about the incident or the harsh words it had caused. Gillian said she couldn't understand what the incident had to do with her request for a favor. Lorna and I tried to explain that not everyone has her truly extraordinary ability to box such explosive incidents up and quickly put them aside.

She was stung by our assessment. "I have to do that," she cried. "I'm in fights with everyone I know everyday. If I couldn't walk away from them, I'd explode!"

> The more I know, the less I understand
> All the things I thought I'd figured out
> I have to learn again
> I've been trying to get down to the heart of the matter
> But everything changes
> and my friends seem to scatter
> But I think it's about forgiveness
> Forgiveness
> Even if, even if you don't love me anymore.

Shortly thereafter, her best friend, B, put a knife into the heart of their relationship when she didn't invite Gillian to her birthday party, causing Gillian to make a final, fervent plea for returning to Redwood for the month of January. I'd been skirting around a final no on the question for weeks, hoping that her pain would ease over Christmas vacation.

Lorna and I had already agreed to get her a horse of her own. Meagan had gotten one when she was eleven, and it was always assumed that one day Gillian would own one, too. Never had the time seemed more appropriate. I also thought

Gillian's despair would be lifted by the prospect of our trip to Europe. Luckily for our finances, the troubled airlines started slashing fares to Europe, enabling me to put four tickets under the Christmas tree.

Gillian was indeed excited about the trip and ecstatic about the idea of having her own horse at long last. But such was the depth of her despondency as the new year approached that she told us, quite sincerely, that she'd rather go back to Redwood than go to Europe and she'd rather have her friends back than a horse.

At the start of the year, I told her that we would go on with the home school. I said I felt deeply sorry about what was happening with her social life, but no more sorry than I felt about what had happened to her academic life a year earlier. I reminded her that all this had come about because in the past she had consistently made decisions in favor of her social life over her academic life, and we were dedicating this year to correcting that imbalance. If, I said, she had complained that she was suffering from an inadequate or improper education at home, that would be a different matter, but we were not going to abandon the home schooling so she could save her friendships. It wouldn't be fair to Redwood, it wouldn't be fair to me, and ultimately it wouldn't be fair to her. I felt sure about my decision, but I knew that if it turned out to be wrong, the Dan Riley School for a Girl and Dan Riley himself would have a heavy burden to carry for a very long time.

For her next writing assignment, I asked her to sum up the first part of the school year. She wrote:

The worst period in my life was the beginning and middle of the 8th grade. I had home studies, and I lost all my friends. Having home studies wasn't the problem. Losing all my friends was what got me down. I was going through one of the hardest times in my life, and I had *no* one to confide in. No one I felt that I could turn to and tell anything, whether it was important or not.

Nothing really changed the situation. I pulled out of my depression by having so much time to myself and taking that time to analyze myself. I have grown tremendously from that innerself finding, but I still wish I had someone else to talk to.

I was badly in need of something to grab on to myself. Those words of hers — "I have grown tremendously from that innerself finding" — would have to be it. It was even less than we had going for us when the home schooling began, when we at least had curiosity. But curiosity was now slowly being eroded by dread: how much worse could things get? Despite my stated determination to carry on, I realized there soon could very well be a point at which we might have to destroy the school to save the girl.

Still, even Gillian was admitting to growth — tremendous growth, in fact. Clutching at that, we pushed on.

The Soviet Union officially broke up during Christmas vacation, which was just as well. I don't think I could have conveyed to Gillian the enormity of this event. For me, it was like learning that cancer had been cured or that car crashes were now a thing of the past. Some of my earliest prayers as a child were that God would protect us from the Russians. The Cuban Missile Crisis had been as much a part of my adolescence as my first time behind the wheel of a car. But what could it possibly mean to a thirteen-year-old in the 1990s? The evils of her world were far too diffuse for her to appreciate the elimination of just one. The Evil Empire was a comforting, comic book notion that recalled a time when the world could be neatly divided into forces of light and dark. An empire of evil, however, was quite another thing — oozing greed, selfishness, and deceit into government, business, church, art, and sport; seeping toxins into our air, water, food, and blood. No, she could not be expected to be impressed with the dissolution of a senile government thousands of miles away. The real threat to her existence was as close as the boy next door.

In a cover story on safe sex, illustrated by a condom, *Newsweek* reported that "health experts warned that the disease [AIDS] could eventually claim more lives than the Korean or Vietnam Wars. Today the death toll from AIDS stands at about 120,000 — more than the two wars combined — and it's still accelerating: more Americans will die of AIDS in the next two years than have died in the past 10." The magazine had arrived in early December. My immediate reaction was, Oh, God, am I going to have to deal with this? Not that I was squeamish about discussing sex with Gillian. I was, rather, simply tired of the whole subject of sex in America. It had become the national obsession — sex on television, sex in music and film; phone sex, computer sex, teenage sex, extramarital sex, old age sex; homosexuals, bisexuals, transsexuals; kinky sex, celibacy, monogamy, bigamy, polygamy; date rape, gang banging, bestiality.

I don't know enough history to know whether there has ever been a culture anywhere to be so immersed in the subject of sex with such grim results. Rather than liberating us, as one might have assumed all this openness would have done, it seems to have made us more sniggering, more rapacious, more phobic, and more confused than ever. Sometimes I'd like to go out and get a T-shirt that says: JUST DO IT AND SHUT UP

ABOUT IT. Maybe we need a national moratorium on the subject for a while — get everyone back into their closets — gays, straights, and everyone in between. Start whispering again. It might help restore some sense of awe to it, some respect, some health.

But this is the old problem of getting the toothpaste back into the tube. It can't be done. Every time I get the idea that I might spirit Gillian off to some out-of-the-way place until the plague passes, I have to remind myself that there are penises in Iowa, too.

My own formal sex education consisted of a CYO talk from our parish priest on saving this very special, unnamed something or other for our future wives; then there was a book my parents gave me when I turned thirteen which referred to everything sexual in the most clinical terms. I read it with a dictionary on my lap, frantically trying to figure out what these mammary glands were that all the girls were supposed to be growing — talk about lost innocence.

Gillian had boyfriends periodically. None seemed to last very long, and happily, none of the relationships seemed terribly intense. Still, I guessed that her sexual knowledge at thirteen was right about where mine was at twenty-five. I didn't resent her knowing more than I, but I was sad that her knowledge came more from survival than fulfillment. Even behind the admonitions about sex in my youth — from priests and fussy clinicians — there had still been the promise of something beautiful to be experienced when one met, fell in love, and eventually made love to that special person. That illusion, too, has dimmed beneath a cloud of depressing divorce statistics and reports of widespread spousal abuse.

I was taught that if you made the wrong sex choices you'd go to hell when you died. Gillian's generation is being told that the hell is a living one; then when they're lucky, they die.

There are some in our society who revel in this dark scenario: the self-denial crowd who see it as a confirmation of their militant sexlessness and the self-indulgent crowd who see it as appropriate for a society they deem hypocritical.

None of that was an immediate issue for me, however. I didn't have to determine how society got to where it was and who was enjoying it and who was suffering from it. All I had to decide was whether reading the article was going to help Gillian swim through those terrible, swift currents out there and should I, therefore, make it an assignment? She was obviously way ahead of me, as shown by her subsequent report:

As I was walking through the kitchen, my attention was caught by large black letters reading SAFE SEX over a silver condom package. Somehow I knew I was going to have to read this article for some assignment in school.

The article was well-written, and was very straight about the facts. There was only one thing that bothered me. An article like that needs to be in a magazine like *Seventeen*. How many teenagers do you know that read *Newsweek*? There needs to be more articles like that in magazines teenagers read: *Surfer, Thrasher, Cosmopolitan, Vogue,* and *Teen.*

Everyone knows about AIDS and safe sex, but unless they're reminded of it, they'll never consider it.

Another big problem is that some people lie. One of the partners may get up enough courage to ask the other person about practicing safe sex, their past relationships and disease. But there's always the danger that the other person may lie if there is anything bad in their past. They may also think they're too cool to practice safe sex or feel offended that their partner thinks that they have a disease or something.

This is a serious issue. I think it should be introduced in

the school system as early as the 5th grade and should be taught by a teacher who really cares or a specialist.

She took no vow of chastity in the paper, but she was appropriately sober and thoughtful. And I was assured that she had a good grasp of the dangers lurking in the sexual waters, which was the least I could expect of the assignment. We could have wrapped up our unit on sex education right there and moved on to the Pythagorean theorem or something, but a package arrived from my mother in Connecticut with a video presentation from one Mike Lange on the subject of abstinence. In her accompanying letter, my mother said that they had tried to get this video shown in the local schools, but, according to her, "the liberals" had gotten it pulled on the grounds of separation of church and state.

At a time when even *Newsweek* was proclaiming that "abstinence may be unrealistic, but it's the only thing that's completely foolproof," I shouldn't have felt terribly square about asking Gillian to watch the video. But my problem, irresponsible as it may sound, was that I didn't have much faith in abstinence as a reliable option for kids, surely not taken alone.

Mere body chemistry makes teenagers not only louder, more restive, and more insecure than adults, but more sexual, too, since it's all so new to them. To expect them to withhold their natural drives for an indefinite period of time has not only struck me as unrealistic but almost cruel. This is especially so since we've created this ersatz period of life between the onset of puberty and the age of eighteen (high school graduation) or twenty-two (college graduation), when the validating pursuits of life — work and making a family — are postponed. In that period, an eternity in the life of a teenager, we expect them to suspend their drives, tend to their studies, and keep quiet. The new puritans among us, like the old, kneel at the altar of that false god Will — will over social forces, will over human nature. Ban the music, censor the movies, and turn off the TV, they believe, and the hormones will fall into single file on their way to responsible adulthood. In my view, it's a simplistic and absolutist response to a difficult and complex problem.

But since virginal daughters are every father's fantasy, I wasn't going to pass up a chance for Gillian to be sold on abstinence. Maybe Mike Lange's video would reach her at a level beyond me. If so, it certainly would make life easier for her and save her from having to master all the necessary tools and strategies if she were to choose otherwise and engage life fully. So, without prologue, I sat her down for an afternoon in front of the video.

Aside from the subject matter, my view of the video itself, having screened it first, was that it was mind-numbing. Lange, a humorless man on a mission, stood before a chalkboard surrounded by the scrubbed, shiny faces of muted teens and marched them inexorably to the dry well of abstinence, where, he promised them, their self-restraint would yield its rewards both in this world and the next. It was clear that if those liberals in Connecticut had not expelled the video from their schools on political grounds, it would have been ousted for its soporific educational technique. Whether this messenger was dooming the message, I'd only learn under the worst of circumstances. After the first hour, Gillian's critique was simple enough: "Do I have to watch all of this?"

In stark contrast to the Mike Lange approach was the Mike Pritchard approach. After their blowup in early December, Lorna assumed the role reserved for her in the home schooling, drawing on her skills as a professional speaker to give

Gillian a communications class on Friday afternoons. One of her sources was *The Power of Choice,* a series of videos by Pritchard, a former juvenile probation officer. His videos are everything Mike Lange's are not. He uses humor effectively, but, more important, the students are full participants in the discussions, which deal openly with not only sexual matters but the whole panoply of teenage concerns: drugs, suicide, relations with parents and friends.

The teenagers in the videos expressed a thoughtfulness and concern for their own lives and the lives of others — a credit to Pritchard, who was wise enough to ask the right questions and really listen to the answers. At the depth of her alienation from her friends, Gillian watched the Pritchard videos with great intensity. It seemed for a time that the kids in the series were serving as her surrogate friends. However, I found it heartbreaking that the communication she craved could only be one way. Pritchard's kids could tell her all about their problems, but she couldn't tell them hers.

One of the videos featured two former best friends who had accidently ended up sitting together during the making of the video, a discussion of friendships. They began describing the breakup of their own friendship in terms that bore an uncanny resemblance to Gillian's falling out with B. During that breakup I'd tried to tell her that, home school or no home school, friendships change during adolescence. I hoped that hearing the same thing from these two girls who'd gone on to other friendships would make a greater impression on her.

After another Pritchard video, about suicide, Gillian and I had our second extended conversation on the subject. She was obviously very interested in it, an interest fueled, she admitted, by the recent suicide attempts by two members of her erstwhile circle of friends. Her fascination and my concern moved me to exhume the two old letters from my former students, Bobby and Doug. Although the letters had had a profound impact on my life and influenced my approach when I returned to teaching after the first two-year stay in California, I'd buried them deep in my memory box. I confess that part of my motivation for deciding to share them with Gillian was vanity. I wanted her to know that once upon a time I had students who opened up to me the way Mike Pritchard's kids opened up to him. More important, however, I wanted Gillian to get as close to this subject as was safe so that she would know the pain involved.

I watched as she read the letters with mounting concern — first Bobby's description of his descent into hell and apparent escape, then Doug's depressing postscript.

"Did you write him?" Gillian asked, turning from Doug's letter, clearly moved.

"I did."

"What did you say?"

I told her I really couldn't remember. I was sure I told him I was shocked, and I was sure I told him I was sorry, but I couldn't remember any specifics — certainly nothing I would have said to make him feel better. "And," I told her, "if I got a letter like that tomorrow, I still don't know what I'd say, because a teenager's suicide doesn't leave you much room for words. The emotions just fill you up too much."

"I feel sorry for Bobby," she said.

"And Doug," I added. "That was fifteen years ago, and he's probably still living with it."

On a happier note, Nigel came into Gillian's life in January. Lorna's communication class fizzled after getting off to a fast start. Lorna was experiencing increasing conflict with her own schedule, and Gillian was less inclined to follow up on assignments that she saw as open-ended. Determined to maintain their own communication if not the class, however, both mother and daughter enthusiastically threw themselves into shopping for a horse on weekends. Lorna was happier with Gillian than she'd been since the home schooling began as the two of them made long trips together in search of the perfect horse. Nigel, a three-year-old chestnut gelding, was the result.

On January 8, Gillian wrote in her journal:

Nigel (KB)
January 3rd, my search for a horse had ended. January 5th, he arrived. My dream horse (with a few flaws that can be fixed). The 16-hand, 3-year-old chestnut was my dream with the personality of a clown. He is my baby — K.B. — he is a Kissing Bandit. The most personable horse. I wish the ring would dry up so I could get on him. He is the best horse in the world and he is all mine.
THANK YOU GOD — and Mom & Dad.

Like it or not (and I'm afraid I was in the latter camp), horse ownership for Gillian was inevitable. My reluctance stemmed from our prior experience with the costs, the risks, and the seemingly interminable horse shows, but we also knew that owning a horse could help Gillian build character and provide her with some badly needed companionship.

Ironically, as wholesome as I think raising horses, or animals in general, is for kids, I don't think anything matches it for heightening a child's sexual awareness or for making them feel comfortable, natural, and curious about their own sexuality. A visit to a stud farm and witnessing a birth — as we had done with Meagan — is as earthy a lesson in sexuality as it gets. Neither of our girls ever needed a dictionary to figure out what was going on. Our experience with Meagan proved that owning a horse works as a diversion from typical teenage pursuits for just so long. When she turned sixteen, her horse, who had been the center of her universe, was left on our doorstep like an abandoned child and she was off, alas, to experience boys, cars, and parties. The same, we expected, would one day happen with Gillian. But even if Nigel bought her only a few years of contentment, he was a bargain.

The following entries from Gillian's journal make clear the critical role Nigel began to play in her life:

JANUARY 9

Things are going pretty well. Well, that is if you focus on the positive things in my life — Nigel. When I really think about my life and analyze it, this is what it looks like:

BAD THINGS

I have no friends. I don't get along with my boyfriend. I only get along with my parents 50% of the time. My sister and I are always fighting. I have home studies. I want to go to Redwood. I'm gaining weight & my room's a mess all the time.

GOOD THINGS

Nigel.

That way it's even.

JANUARY 15

Well, A and I broke up, and I hate him now. I feel like I have nothing. He was my last social connection. Nigel is the only thing that makes me happy now. I try to spend most of my time with him so I am always in joyful spirits. I long 4 my friends at Redwood, but am appreciative of my new found friend/gift.

P.S. HAPPY BIRTHDAY
MARTIN LUTHER KING

JANUARY 17

I love Fridays still even though I used to love them because I could stay at home all day and sleep in. I still love
them. I look forward to spending the whole day at the barn.
I feel like that is my home away from home. It's the place
that I go when I want to escape and forget. It's only down
the street and I'm not escaping much, but it's like when I
see my horse and hear his soft nicker that he's glad to see
me, everything is erased in my mind until I can't see his
head poking out the door, waving goodbye.

JANUARY 22

I love my horse. I have never been so proud of anything
in the world, especially owning anything this special. I get
complimented on him wherever [we] go. He is so good. I
love him. If I could, I would live down there, then I would
never be sad or lonely again. He has come into my life at a
time of insecurity for both of us, and together we will pull
out of it.

Whether it was the horse alone, the realization that returning to Redwood was not an option, the Pritchard tapes, the
fuller integration of Lorna into her life, a combination of all
the above, or an unknown that completely escaped my powers of observation, I don't know, but I do know that Gillian
definitely began to "pull out of it." She was slowly but surely
emerging as a happier human being, and thus a better student.

On January 27 we reached the halfway point in our school
year. It was the occasion for a reflective conversation. Joseph
Campbell had been the most significant discovery of my seminary studies back in the early seventies, and Lorna relied

heavily on his work in her seminars. It is an article of faith with both of us that Campbell's hero's journey, wherein the individual is separated from the comforts of home and forced to confront the demons of his or her world alone, is essential to realizing one's full human potential. We had conducted endless dinner table conversations about this journey while our children, especially Gillian, listened — rather heroically themselves — off to the side.

But as Gillian and I reflected on the time that had just transpired, with special attention to the hellish period she had most recently endured, I realized that she had made something of a hero's journey herself. As essential as I believe the journey to be, I never would have planned it as part of our curriculum. I never would have consciously subjected Gillian to the heartache and isolation she experienced. Much of what happened was by accident; it happened because of my inability to foresee all the possible outcomes. But since it did happen, I wanted Gillian to embrace her experience and accept it as a necessary and vital part of growing up.

Gillian was remarkably responsive to this characterization of her ordeal. I think for the first time, after sitting in a haze through all those conversations, the hero's journey finally made some sense to her. Surely none of Campbell's archetypal heroes could have described their experiences any more vividly than she did in her journal on February 9:

I haven't written in so long because nothing has changed really. The nights are short and the days crawl by slowly. Although I would never tell anyone I was glad about going through home studies, and I will never deny the pain which I have spoken of and the unwritable feelings that just can't be recorded, I will say that I have grown a lot from this experience. I feel like a new vine that has grown from a seed of pain. I will never forget this year, and I am sure I have much further to grow. I will never see what I used to be and I am far from what I will be. I am still lost in black, but now I am aware.

The insight, optimism, and new resolve she was beginning to express in our daily lessons was reflected in this paper that I asked her to write about her hopes for 1992.

Thank God I had just finished a depression right before the beginning of the new year. It's always nice to start off the year on the right foot. Here are some of my plans.

First of all, I truly believe your whole outlook on life is based completely on your attitude. I would like to become a more positive thinker (that way life won't seem so bad). In the summer I will devote my mornings to my brand new baby, and the rest of the day to rebuilding lost friendships.

With the school-filled part of my life, well I don't really have any goals or anything. I would just like to remember that I'm going to be here for the rest of the year so I might as well make the best of it.

With Nigel I have decided that I would like to advance with my riding skills, at the end of the year be in a steady state of progression, almost perfected ground manners, and ready to take on the competition at E.T.I. [Equestrian Trails, Inc.].

I'm not really going to worry about the friend aspect of my life until summer when I can do something about it. For now, all I can do is wait, try not to make things worse, and hope that in developing a warm personality I can melt their ice wall.

Basically I want to be a perfect person by the end of the year! Is that asking too much?

~ 7 ~

THE THIRD QUARTER

EVEN WITH GILLIAN'S SPIRITS REVIVED, the dawn of the
third quarter found me no less anxiety-ridden than I had been
at the beginning of the first and second. Only now my concern
was whether I was going to have enough time to teach her all
the things I still had planned.

I wanted us to do an astronomy project together. There was
much left to do in math — we hadn't even touched on algebra
or geometry yet. We had the trip to Europe coming up, and
with it the need to get a grip on a few foreign languages. (We
had divided up the tongues of the three countries on our
itinerary — Meagan would handle the Spanish, Lorna the
French, and Gillian and I would take care of the Italian.)
A presidential primary was in progress, although the tabloid
elements of it had persuaded me to wait until it started to
take on some educational value by resembling the democratic
process rather than an afternoon in front of *Geraldo*. And
there was spelling.

Persistently, since early in the first quarter, I had succeeded
slightly in raising Gillian's consciousness about spelling. I was
beginning to get papers in which she was correcting misspellings on her own. This was a considerable improvement over
her early papers, which could very well have been written in
Italian for all the semblance they bore to English. Truly, the

girl who had raised the question in early childhood about why we just didn't spell "why" as "y" had become a spelling anarchist. As reassuring as her efforts may have been, the sheer volume of her misspellings exceeded her patience and drove me to despair, made more acute by my own guilt at having contributed to her reckless spelling habits.

In the second grade, Gillian had written the following paper:

THE HALLOWEEN STOY
One nithed all the Halloween cariters came into the dark. My fafrit was the gost. Then the gost became rilae. I saide can we be frends. The gost saide ok but as loing as you do not tel inne bute then I wel not tel inne bute. I wel not tel inne bute as loing as you do not scker inne of my frends. Ok saide the gost. My gost frends mit make frunt of you. OK I saide del del ok.
    The End

Her teacher expected parents to help correct their children's errors before the papers were collected. Rather than doing just that, like a responsible parent, I broadcast my immense amusement with the paper to one and all. I read it to everyone who walked in the house. I made photocopies of it and sent it to grandparents. And I wrote the following note to Gillian's teacher:

Mrs. P,
We hav pruf red Gillian's stoy just lyk you ast and it luks just fyn to us.
    The Rileys

Mrs. P gave Gillian an A+ on the paper, so between us we had combined to send her the wrong message about bad spelling. I'll never know if that seemingly harmless little incident was entirely responsible, but Gillian's spelling had remained pretty much at the level of the *gost* paper.

Spelling was a rather sensitive issue with me, since I'd once launched a political career in New Hampshire over it. A parent had become incensed because his daughter was writing letters to her grandparents filled with misspellings. As her English teacher, he concluded, I was to blame. I tried to explain that I was one of many teachers she'd had in her schooling and that not all my students wrote poorly spelled letters to their grandparents. But he was riding high on the incompetence-of-public-school-teachers bandwagon, and there was no stopping him from claiming his spot on the school board.

So I knew what would be in store for me if the press ever got its hands on one of Gillian's papers; the Dan Riley School for a Girl would be exposed as a sham, and I would be dodging embarrassing interviews on my doorstep in my robe and slippers.

Therefore, in the third quarter I rededicated myself to her spelling. We did daily exercises, reviewed the basic rules, made lists of words, and through the career of John Sununu observed the consequences of poor spelling in later life. When Sununu's letter of resignation as the White House chief of staff appeared in the newspaper, a misspelling was duly noted. "I assure you that in pit bull mode or pussey [*sic*] cat mode I am ready to help," Sununu had written.

"See that *sic*," I warned Gillian. "That's what you get when you misspell something in public. It's like having a scarlet letter on your chest, only the letter is *M* for Misspeller."

But, Gillian pointed out, Sununu's inability to spell did not prevent him from achieving some measure of success in his life. Indeed, he had taught at Dartmouth, governed New

Hampshire, and served at the right hand of the president. As this incident, and later the vice president's inability to spell "potato," would confirm, poor spelling isn't much of an obstacle to attaining wealth or power in America. Gillian's obvious grasp of that fact wouldn't make our progress any easier.

Much of my desperation at this time was due to my realization that our school probably wasn't going to last beyond the eighth grade. I didn't really know how long it would last when we started, but given the difficulties of the second quarter, I didn't expect it to be in operation the next September. So I was anxious, not only to squeeze in as much learning as possible, but to start laying plans for Gillian's freshman year in high school. To this end we started to investigate private schools.

Gillian was ambivalent. I assured her that she would have more of a say in her schooling for the ninth grade than she had had for the eighth. To ensure her full cooperation, we agreed to approach the process as a lesson in preparing and applying for institutional acceptance. The main objective, I told her, was not to get into a private school but to learn about filling out applications, meeting standards, making deadlines, visiting campuses, and being interviewed.

At her first interview, I was a wreck. As detached as I tried to be, I still fell back into the trap of thinking that this wasn't a sovereign person presenting herself to this school but an extension of myself — more than ever now that I was claiming responsibility for her formal education for the past six months. I fought mouth dryness and head lightness as the interview began. The headmaster asked Gillian what she was looking for in a school. Gillian shrugged her shoulders and replied, "I don't know. One school's the same as another, I guess." She said it straightforwardly and without attitude, but it was not the right answer. The right answer was, "I'm look-ing for a school that will challenge me and help me meet my potential as a student and productive citizen of the world."

Were Gillian Charley McCarthy and I Edgar Bergen, that is the answer she would have given. Alas, that was not the case. We were Gillian and her father, separate and equal. I just squirmed in my seat and smiled a lame smile that said, "Kids. Huh?"

The admissions director then asked Gillian what her goals were. If she'd shrugged her shoulders and answered, "I don't know. One goal is the same as another," I think I would have run from the room, howling. Instead, unpredictable as ever, she launched into an earnest, detailed plan for her future. She said that first she was going to go to Notre Dame and get a law degree. Then she was going to go to work for her mom so she could sharpen her speaking and sales skills. Then she was going to save the rain forest and host a talk show. And then, when she was about thirty-five, she was going to run for governor of California, then president of the United States.

Charley McCarthy lives!

No, that was unfair. I never would have had the nerve or the imagination to make a reach like that. It was not only breath-taking in its scope, but rather sophisticated in its delineation of the steps that might be necessary on such a career path.

I really do believe that parents should be satisfied with the basics in their children's lives — health and happiness, but I must admit I craved a scene like that one. I was puffed up to dizzying heights as I floated above the room on the wings of Gillian's ambition. I was Henry Higgins on the verge of song: "I think she's got it. By Jove, I think she's got it."

Gillian, my child who had spent so much time at war with her best self, who (like the young and immature everywhere) had a view of the world limited to the here and now, was beginning to say yes to her talents, intelligence, energy, and future. In all my years of working with youth, nothing was clearer to me than this: acknowledging his or her role in the future was the most significant turning point in a kid's life. Once a youth is able to project self into a future of consequence, all the other choices — about drugs, sex, studies, citizenship, relationships — become, if not always right, at least reasoned. The callow selfishness that marks the infantile drive for instant gratification ceases to dominate, and the human being makes an essential connection with time. I felt that I had had the rare privilege of being present at that turning point in my daughter's life.

On our way home, we stopped off for lunch. Gillian brought a burger, fries, a milkshake, and an apple turnover to the table; I brought materials from the school — the student newspaper, a brochure, course descriptions, a financial aid form. As Gillian ate, I continued to bubble as I reviewed all the highlights of the school. She listened politely through her burger, but between sips of the shake she said, "It's very far away from Nigel. I don't know how I'd ever have time for riding him."

Gillian had me on a yo-yo again — and I was on the way down. Of the schools we were going to be seeing, this one was the closest. If the entire decision was going to turn on her time with Nigel, an issue I hadn't even considered, there was no point in looking at the other schools.

With undisguised disappointment, I thumbed through the materials in front of me. "Well, let's see how much money you're going to save us by not going to this school," I said, taking out my pen.

She blew into the steam from her turnover. "I didn't say I didn't want to go," she said. "I just haven't made up my mind yet."

The yo-yo was on the way back up.

Interestingly enough, the magical moment of the school interview made it impossible to continue to ignore the decidedly unmagical presidential primary. Its very tawdriness, which had forced me to exclude it from our studies in the beginning, was making it a compelling issue for us to discuss. The sex, drug, and draft questions that swirled around Bill Clinton during the New Hampshire primary echoed the belated sexual harassment charges leveled against Clarence Thomas the previous fall. Only by being viewed in a nonpartisan way, I believed, was it possible to truly weigh a question Gillian raised. After expressing astonishment that Clinton was having to answer for a letter he'd written to his draft board eighteen years earlier, she asked, "What would make it impossible for me to ever become president?" Then, to make clear that she was talking about childhood crimes, she added, "Like what if I ever got thrown out of school?"

Gillian had quickly gone from projecting herself into a future of consequence to projecting herself into a future of consequences. In an instant I realized the razor-sharp line between the two. I wanted her to understand consequences. I wanted her to appreciate the need to answer for her actions, but what was transpiring on the national stage, clearly enough for a thirteen-year-old to see, was the Orwellian specter of cradle-to-grave accountability.

And the new puritans are an unforgiving lot. Like their forebears, they're quick with the branding iron — an A seared to the chest for Adulterer, an SH for Sexual Harasser, PS for Pot Smoker. Gum Chewer. Bed Wetter. Misspeller. Indeed, one national columnist even attacked Clinton for showing unseemly ambition as a fifteen-year-old for wanting to be president — O for Overreacher.

I did not want to mislead Gillian. My sense was that things

were getting worse. As the battle lines were being drawn more sharply and the new puritans from both the left and right were wielding more and more influence over the national agenda, tolerance, understanding, acceptance, and forgiveness of human frailties was in precipitous decline. But I did not want her to cringe at the sight of the future just when she had come to see herself in it. So I told her I still thought anybody could overcome anything in this country with sincerity, hard work, and good intentions. I didn't know if that was true, but I did not want her to anticipate a future in which it was not.

Although we were emphasizing math and spelling in the third quarter, we were not abandoning the reading component of our program. Gillian had already demonstrated that she was a good reader, and the best thing I could do for her was to get her in the habit of reading every day. To start the quarter, I offered her a choice of two books: Anne Morrow Lindbergh's *Gift from the Sea* and Joyce Maynard's *Looking Backward,* either of which I thought might inspire her journal writing.

When I taught the Who Am I course at Lebanon High School in the seventies, I'd had some success using *Looking Backward,* written when Maynard was seventeen. I thought that would be the book that Gillian would choose. But after sampling chapters from both books, she surprised me and chose Lindbergh's paean to solitude and contemplation, a book written in the fifties by an older woman, a wife and mother. Her choice forced me to go back and review both books myself. When I did, her decision seemed less surprising.

The quality of the Maynard book that had attracted my students and me was its immediacy, its relevance — that most inflated value of those days. But in 1992 all those references to the Beatles and the Vietnam War were, for Gillian, no more relevant than a discourse on Gregorian chants or the Peloponnesian War. What obviously worked better were timeless reflections in nature on a woman's role and destiny as a person. And *Gift from the Sea* had the most wonderful effect on Gillian. I'd find her curled up with it on the floor of the living room where a patch of sunlight spread itself out each morning, the mystic music of Enya playing softly in the background.

One day we were about to do math when she broke one of our cardinal rules by putting on music. I told her to take it off immediately. In mock melodramatic fashion she exclaimed, "Dad, you have not read *Gift from the Sea*. I can't exist in a vacuum. I need fuel for my soul. Music is the fuel of my soul!" She went on to explain how the music worked in keeping her attention where it belonged. She said her attention was always drifting. If there was no music, she started playing with her fingernails or looking off in the distance. The music, she maintained, kept her focused on the subject. She might dance away from the subject briefly, she said, but the rhythm of the music always brought her back to it.

I loved her use of reason — such an improvement over the ranting and raving of bygone days. I loved, too, the reference to *Gift from the Sea*. I told her I loved all of this, that I took it as a sign of maturity and learning. Then I told her to turn the music off, and we continued with our math.

Without any prompting from me, the book began to make its way directly and indirectly into her journal:

MARCH 6
Ever since I started reading *Gift from the Sea,* I have been dreaming of being alone. Not like I'm not now. But . . . well, I don't know. It's weird.

MARCH 27 "THE MIND"
How does it work? The thoughts and ideas, values and morals . . . they are all there in your mind, but are distorted

with time. When we were young, the smallest things interested us . . . a butterfly, a flower, a blade of grass. As we got older, bigger, "better" things caught our attention — a black BMW . . . a bottle of the best wine, Picasso's greatest, a big house and a whole beach to keep us happy and surrounded by beautiful, wonderful things.

What happened to the butterfly that could flutter by and keep a smile on your face all day? It is gone, distorted with time, hidden somewhere far in the mind.

What if everyone took some time to go back and renew the old? Go back to the simplicity they used to know as a child.

How would you do that? What would it be like? Is it like Anne Morrow Lindbergh and *Gift from the Sea*?

APRIL 3

I appreciate being alive today more than I did yesterday. Every day you learn a tiny bit more and then it hits you. You say look at how far I've come. Look at all I know. I remember being in kindergarten and watching someone handwrite. I thought, I will never be able to do that, especially since I could barely get through my ABCs. Now I can write anything in script with every letter formed perfectly and say my ABCs frontwards and backwards.

I seem to go through these bursts every once in a while where I feel so knowledgeable I just want to talk to someone about something of a higher level than boys and what we're doing on Friday night.

Oddly enough, this decidedly prefeminist work of Lindbergh's planted the buds of some feminist thinking in Gillian's head. Feminism per se had never been part of our curriculum, mostly because I find it confusing. In November, for instance, the *L.A. Times* had carried two dispatches on subsequent days from the feminist front. The first was about the decision by a female judge in New York to overturn the convictions of ten women cited for exposing their breasts in public to protest the legal distinction between male and female breasts. The second was about the successful attempt by a female college professor at Penn State to have the nude woman in a reproduction of Goya's *Naked Maja* removed from a classroom wall because its presence constituted sexual harassment. If I were "teaching" feminism to Gillian, I really wouldn't know which story indicated progress. Perhaps they both did, but if so, I couldn't explain how, because they seemed to be pushing in opposite directions.

More to the point, though, I didn't build feminism into the curriculum because basically I just don't buy it. It has always seemed to me to be one more attempt to segment, fragment, throw up walls, and frame all thought, talk, and action in terms of them versus us. A primary objective in raising both Meagan and Gillian had been to instill in them a sense of personal dignity and self-worth — which would have been the same goal had they been born boys. I wanted them to be aware that — like the very tall or short or fat, like blacks or Jews or gays, like people with lisps or southern accents, people with very high or low I.Q.'s, people who had been abused as children and people who had been indulged as children, people, in short, who had the misfortune to be born into this world as human beings — they would face certain disadvantages in society. And I wanted them to recognize that there are numerous tools, strategies, sources of information, and support groups for helping them overcome or at least neutralize those disadvantages. But I never wanted either of them to subordinate her greater identity as human being to the lesser identity as a member of an interest group.

What has emerged as a result are two people whom, I suspect, most feminists would be comfortable in calling sisters — proud, passionate, purposeful about their place in society. During the Clarence Thomas hearings, neither my aversion to feminism nor their having been raised in a humanist as opposed to feminist environment prevented them from arriving at firm, clear conclusions on the significance of that event: that sexual harassment was an insidious problem in the workplace long overdue for serious national debate; that the Senate reflected chiefly a straight, white, middle-age, male point of view; and that Anita Hill, whatever the unfairness to Thomas, was probably the more truthful of the two. The gratifying thing about those conclusions was that they were reached by a long, lively debate among the four independent human beings in our house, not by unleashing some fierce, bare-toothed dogma.

MARCH 17

My birthday. I figured the day would come and go without me even realizing it. Just like "Sixteen Candles," except I would be the one who forgot. It's not like I had something else important weighing on my mind or anything. I just didn't have anything to really be happy about or look forward to — or so I thought. All my presents had been bought and given to me weeks before because I was in desperate need of them and couldn't wait until my birthday.

I know receiving isn't supposed to be the key thing in any holiday or special occasion. It's supposed to be love and being together and all that stuff. But I, at 13, had not learned to fully appreciate the non-materialistic things in my life yet.

The day started with warm family greetings, happy B-days, and my favorite breakfast. Then we proceeded with school. I had already gotten a couple of H B-day calls from friends in the morning and only expected to get a few more later that night. That's where I was wrong. People called me that I didn't even think had my phone #. I was glad to hear old voices I used to know so well, and, of course, the ones fresh in my memory. So this was the day I learned to appreciate just the love around me and be completely satisfied.

Not only did the entry reveal that she had not been abandoned by her friends, but it also showed her recent growth as both person and student. This growth was being reflected in all our work. She was doing her math assignments conscientiously, sparing me the usual preliminaries about my questionable competence in the subject, or comparisons with what her friends were doing at Redwood, or how fast or how slowly we should be advancing. She cheerfully followed me on our march through the rules of spelling, even through the swamplands where I'd lost students in the past — *i before e except after c, and except in* seize, *which may sound like* siege *but is not spelled like it.*

Her participation in our study of the morning paper became more active. She started to gush questions much as she had as a two-year-old, recapturing, in this regard at least, part of the wonderment of childhood that in her journal she had lamented losing. Even a presidential trip to Japan, equally burdened by the denseness of the trade imbalance issue and the unseemliness of George Bush's vomiting episode, elicited a flurry of questions: Why don't we just study how the Germans and Japanese do it and do what they do? Who made that car in *Back to the Future*? Why'd he try to do it on his own? Why didn't he try to get somebody else to help him make it? Why'd he only do it in one color? Did Iacocca pay off his loan to the government? Why doesn't he go back for another loan if things are so bad again? Who makes BMWs and Mercedeses? Do Germans make any cheap, plastic cars? Who makes Lamborghinis? How about Ferraris? So Italians only make cars for about forty rich people, huh?

We were getting at what was for me the essence of the student-teacher relationship: the imagination and curiosity of the student unlocked; the teacher as resource and guide.

The impact of this great change in Gillian was also reflected in our investigation into private schools. She became not just a willing participant but an enthusiastic one. The main object of her enthusiasm was the Thacher School in Ojai, California. Its appeal was summed up in the following line from its catalogue: "Each freshman is required to keep a horse for his or her first year . . ."

For the first time since she first walked into a school almost a decade before, Gillian was genuinely excited about the idea of school. My own enthusiasm was somewhat restrained by the price tag on a Thacher education, but this was what I had wanted, this was what I had been working toward: Gillian's rejuvenation as a student. I couldn't dampen it now over something like $20,000 per year in tuition — even if it was almost twice as much as I'd ever made as a teacher, even if it was close to the cost of a year at Harvard, Yale, or Stanford. Besides, I told myself, we were only window shopping.

Gillian diligently filled out the five-page application for Thacher, studied for the three-hour entrance exam, and drove 40 miles north with me for an interview. She did all of this even though we knew that Thacher had already sent out its acceptances for the following school year and that our only chance for her admission was for one of those acceptances to decline. The Gillian of an earlier incarnation would have squandered her emotions and energies arguing about what a monumental waste of time it all was. The new Gillian was as impressed with Thacher as the old dad was. It was neither a waste of time nor would it be a waste of money, for it seemed a truly utopian school. Not only was it rich in all the facilities that money could buy — tennis courts, shiny new library, plush student lounge, outdoor amphitheater, individual dormitory rooms — all surrounded by acres of woods, fields, and streams, but it seemed to have an almost otherworldly spirit of community.

Gillian and I watched a regular Friday morning assembly from different vantage points. A grandmotherly librarian read an article from a professional library journal on the importance of the First Amendment. A student announced a bonfire dance for the next night. Another student read a letter he'd written to President Bush, urging him to attend the environmental summit conference in Rio; he said he'd pin the letter to the bulletin board for all interested parties to sign. Two students with a boom box cajoled the grandmotherly librarian into helping them sell the students on a reggae party in the lounge. A history teacher offered an analysis of the recently held British election. Someone else sorted out some esoteric cafeteria business.

Everyone listened — respectfully when respect was called for; cheerily when it was not. It all seemed so remarkable for a gathering of Americans — of any age group — in our contentious society. I wondered whether or not such civility was itself becoming a luxury in America, available only to the privileged few. And I wondered, too, just how far in life Gillian could go, educated in such a paradise as this.

As we made our way down the mountain road from Thacher, Gillian looked back at it in awe and said, "That is one fine school."

At that instant I would've paid twice the tuition to get her into a school that could inspire that kind of admiration. But money was not the issue; it was effectively out of our hands. We could only wait and see if some other applicant rejected Thacher and then if Thacher accepted Gillian.

Meanwhile, we would pack our bags and head for Europe.

FIELD TRIP

ONLY IN AMERICA IN 1992 could a trip to Europe be freighted with the baggage of five hundred years of history, especially if that trip involved the two places most associated with Christopher Columbus — Spain and Genoa. The first history I learned as a schoolboy in the orderly fifties was that in 1492 a brave Italian seaman named Christopher Columbus, sailing under the flag of Spain, discovered America and proved that the world was round. When I was reintroduced to Columbus in college in the sixties, he had, as the iconoclasm of the day dictated, been reduced to a blundering knave, like a character off Gilligan's island, barely able to navigate his way around the Mediterranean, let alone discover a new world. As we planned our itinerary in the blame-assigning nineties, Columbus was being cast yet again, now as a seafaring genocidal maniac bent on exterminating the indigenous peoples of the New World with a horrific array of weapons, diseases, and insults.

The Columbus Gillian learned about at the Dan Riley School for a Girl, where propaganda was frowned on, would be none of these. I discussed the differing interpretations of Columbus with her in terms of what they told us about the variable nature of historical "knowledge" and about the times in which such views became popular.

I think that speculations on the character or intentions of long-dead historical figures make for amusing parlor games but are of dubious value for underpinning a true knowledge of history. Meagan and Gillian have grown up in an atmosphere in which John F. Kennedy is best known as the victim of a wide-ranging conspiracy encompassing numerous arms of the U.S. government, foreign agents, mafia hitmen, and a gang of cross-dressers . . . or as the primary suspect in the Marilyn Monroe murder case. Although most of the historians who have written about Kennedy lived during his lifetime, the portrait of him continues to be revised. Columbus lived half a millennium ago; the firsthand record on him is sparse by comparison. How can there be any more certainty whether he was a man with courage in his heart or murder?

Such speculations become downright destructive when they are used to inflame new animosities among people or keep alive the embers of past hostilities. A protest had erupted in Pasadena in December when the Rose Bowl Committee chose a descendant of Columbus to be grand marshal of the Rose Parade. Not only had Columbus been found guilty by the most hysterical reading of the evidence, but, like Adam, who had sullied the first Eden, his sin would be visited upon his progeny for generations to come. The new puritans had struck again.

I did not ask Gillian to "learn" whether Columbus was brave or barbaric. I asked her to learn the facts as both his defenders and detractors would agree upon them:

WHO: Christopher Columbus, Genovese seaman
WHAT: Opened the Americas up to western Europe
WHEN: 1492
WHERE: Crossing the Atlantic with three ships, the *Niña*, the *Pinta*, and the *Santa Maria*

WHY: Searching for a shorter route to India
How: Accidentally landed in a place he called the West Indies

That, I felt, would be useful and enduring knowledge for Gillian, and she wouldn't have to be ashamed of it when she got to college. Of course, she still might be made to feel guilty for engaging in such Eurocentric behavior as traveling to Europe. But I was optimistic that the new puritans would lose their place on the national stage in due time and that voices of reason and common sense would eventually prevail.

Such voices would have been welcome on our trip, too. But to that tormenting question travelers love to ask themselves when it's too late — what did we forget? — reason and common sense could very well have been our answer.

This was planned as a learning trip for the whole family, especially for Gillian. She would be exchanging money, converting miles to kilometers, speaking foreign languages, viewing great art, and touching historic landmarks. Our school on wheels would travel from Barcelona to Provence, the French Riviera, Genoa, and the Italian Riviera. All that, but only if we could get out of the airport parking lot in Spain.

I could not find reverse in our rental car, and imbued, I guess, with the machismo that comes with suddenly being in the land of matadors and conquistadors, I refused to ask for help, which greatly helped to exacerbate the tensions that had begun fourteen hours earlier, when we had gotten a late start to Los Angeles International, got stuck in rain-swollen traffic, boarded our plane five minutes before takeoff, and then, through my own foolishness, got separated in Atlanta on our way to our connecting flight. The tension did not ease up much when Lorna unilaterally decided to seek help from the rental agent, nor when he demonstrated that putting the car in reverse required a movement as stealthy as any in those James Bond cars that eject passengers or spread wings and fly.

We didn't fare much better in first, second, or third gears. Driving in Barcelona brought back memories of the chariot race in *Ben Hur*, only he had the advantage of simply driving in a circle. We were trying to go places — Montjuic, the Gothic Quarter, Eixample. I drove; Lorna navigated; we warred continuously. She was constantly telling me to get into right lanes, which always seemed to fill up with buses quicker than I could fill up with nerve. We were pushed from behind by armies of dragsters. And always, everywhere, we were surrounded by gnatlike motor scooters. When we pulled up on a sidewalk and tried to figure out how to turn on the headlights, Spaniards, Catalans, and even Basque Separatists united in condemning us with blaring horns, flashing lights, and that international sign of welcome: the middle finger salute.

It was then that I snapped at Gillian for the crime of back-seat driving — a capital crime, it seemed to me under the circumstances. If I'd been a dog, she'd have been without a face. The loss of face, as it turned out later, was all mine, however. I was sure that I had ruined the entire trip in the first twenty-four hours. But Gillian's journal entry at the end of the day indicated that my daughter, at least, had not left her sense of proportion behind.

MARCH 24

Well, the trip here was long and everyone is beat. But the city is beautiful. It looks like a combination of Boston, New York, Mexico and something out of the old middle times.

Of course we had the usual Riley family crises and nerv- ous breakdowns, starting early Monday morning and continuing up to dinner Tuesday night in Barcelona. I have no doubt that there will be more, but maybe less when we all get some real sleep.

Gillian's newfound maturity was not always in evidence, however. Like the rest of us, the clothes she'd packed were foolishly weighted toward California lights and whites. Unlike the rest of us, though, who quickly bowed to the bite of the Spanish spring air and donned parkas, Gillian persisted in wearing T-shirts and shorts. This gave Spaniards who had missed the opportunity to laugh at us behind the wheel of our car the chance to ridicule us as we strolled along the boulevards — often briskly. The American teenager's allegiance to a peculiar fashion and a willingness to withstand the taunts and admonitions of adults in any language are surely marvels of human nature.

MARCH 25

Two days in Barcelona and so far the best thing is MTV. Just kidding.

Driving in the city has made some people go crazy. I won't mention any names, Dad. The city is truly beautiful . . . well, what I've seen when I've been able to keep my eyes open. The jet lag is taking its toll on me.

Appropriately enough, one of the things that saved us — in Barcelona, anyway — was a statue of Columbus. There he stood, looking over the water with his outstretched hand pointing west . . . west from Connecticut to California, all the places we had called home. Montjuic was over his right shoulder, the Ramblas and our hotel directly behind him, the Picasso Museum over his left shoulder. Columbus the statue — doing all that we could ever ask of a historical figure — showing us where we've been and helping us get where we want to go.

By the time we reached France, I'd given up any pretense at formal classes for Gillian. Sleep was scarce, the drives were long, and the sheer energy required to keep up with the traffic, count up the change for the countless tolls, and make all the right turns left no time to discuss the Renaissance or conduct Italian lessons in the car. This change in agenda was not lost on Meagan, who, since becoming a highly disciplined and motivated college student, had emerged as the last skeptic of the home school. "Isn't she going to have to learn anything on this trip," Meagan asked, "or is this going to be one of those absorption things?"

"She's going to absorb," I answered, feeling both guilty and defeated. For the first time since the home schooling experiment had begun, I was overwhelmed by the dual responsibilities of teacher and father. More than once in the past couple of days I'd muttered to myself, "I want a dad, too."

An easier, more practical way of making this trip, of course, would have been to join a tour group, board a bus each morning, and let an expert guide us through the historic sights. But the easier, more practical way of educating Gillian that year would have been to enroll her in public school again. It just wasn't to be a year for easier, more practical ways of doing things. Besides, Lorna and I had traveled like this once before. In the early eighties, we had gone to Italy with nothing more than a guidebook, willing to simply lose ourselves in a foreign culture for a while and take our chances on what we would learn about it and ourselves. The revelations on both counts were worth the frustrations, and I had hoped that we could replicate that experience.

Three days after our arrival, the trip attained the quality

of joy for the first time in St-Rémy-de-Provence when we took a room in the Château de Roussan, formerly owned by the family of Nostradamus. The château had comfortably settled into the eighteenth century and was clearly not going to be budged out of it by the addition of swimming pools, tennis courts, gift shops, restaurants, or new paint. As the restaurants in town were closed, we sought out dinner in a grocery store, returning to our room with all the makings for one of those meals Americans dream of having in France — heavenly bread, tasty wine, delectable cheese, and olives lusty in shape, smell, and succulence. A heavy rain on the old roof proved a pleasant substitute for the stereophonic sounds that normally accompanied our meals and complemented the ambience.

We sat around — just our family of four — listening to the rain, eating, and talking well into the night in a room near where the young Nostradamus may have decided it would be easier to predict the future than to remember the past. Our own recent, frantic past was not as dizzying to contemplate anymore, and we could laugh about our frenzied departure from the States, the fear of death and embarrassment on the streets of Barcelona, and the evil that lurks in the hearts of loved ones who haven't gotten enough sleep.

We toasted Meagan, who had gotten us through Spain with her meager but hard-earned Spanish vocabulary, faltering only when we tried to order decaffeinated coffee. Our waiter called the maître d' for assistance. "Ah, decaffinado!" he declared. We toasted Lorna, who had turned her high school French, a few strategic hand gestures, and a generous helping of smiles into a dialogue with Brigitte, the plump and cheery clerk of the château who knew not a word of English. And they all toasted me for plowing through enough travel books to find this gem of a resting place — a welcome balm to my badly bruised ego.

Gillian was subjected to a good-natured kidding about her wardrobe, which prompted her to ask what *C'est la vie* meant. It was interesting that those were the first French words she ever spoke. I'd have preferred *liberté, egalité, fraternité,* or even *L'addition, s'il vous plaît!,* but for an American teenager, *C'est la vie* is probably the most useful French expression.

The next morning we visited the Ruines de Glanum; that afternoon we toured the Palais des Papes in Avignon, and that evening we strolled along the magnificent cours Mirabeau in Aix-en-Provence. Surely at such a pace the absorption approach to learning wasn't going to be any better than the formal approach. My planning had turned Gillian into a moving target; a sponge would have had a better chance to absorb so much history and culture.

Fortunately, the pace slowed down considerably when we reached Italy — where else? — and for a few days the only thing any of us had to absorb was the sea and sun. Gillian was appreciative and quite reflective as a result.

MARCH 28

Today was probably the best, our first real day in Italy, but already I can tell it's beautiful. We walked two and a half miles down to Portofino from Santa Margherita. It was all next to the ocean, some of the most gorgeous water I've ever seen. There were people snorkling and scuba diving all along the way.

There is a difference from country to country, even though they're within a few hours of each other. The people talk different, act different, and look different. It's a completely different atmosphere.

To clear up a myth about the French — they are extremely helpful and kind people, at least all the ones that
we met.

MARCH 29

Now that I think about it, this will be the longest our
family has been together with no little breaks. When you
are with people or a person for an extreme amount of time,
you begin to notice many annoyances and the smallest
things start to magnify by the millions. Because our family
does not spend masses amount of time together on a regular
basis we were not very good at — how should I say? —
"getting along," "compromising," "getting out of the attack mode." But eventually we got better.

I am definitely the hardest to get along with, and then we
sort of go in pairs. My sister and I argue a lot because we
are together more. She also has not learned to put up with
my "personality" as much as everyone else. Mom and
Dad/teacher argue a lot because they play the roles of driver
and navigator, but they don't argue as much as they should,
and they have gotten much better at it, as have Meagan
and I.

As if our plate wasn't full enough, we met a young American at a restaurant in Santa Margherita one night who persuaded us to add Florence to our itinerary. Lorna and I
had been to Florence on our earlier trip to Italy. We loved
Florence, but even I had the good sense to realize that adding
the Uffizi Gallery, the Palazzo Pitti, and the Bargello to the
syllabus was sure to invite death by culture. Besides, I knew if
we ventured farther south, we'd never have time for Genoa on
our return trip. But we'd already gotten a glimpse of it from
the autostrada, and the girls were not impressed. Columbus or
no Columbus, they were happy to swap Genoa for Florence.

In Florence we stood in line at the Galleria dell'Accademia to see Michelangelo's *David*. Meagan joked that she had already seen the one in Las Vegas. Gillian didn't get it until we explained that there were copies of *David* everywhere, including one of those ridiculous theme casinos in Las Vegas, which prompted her to joke, "So, if there are so many free fakes of it all over the place, why are we standing in line to pay to see this one?"

To Gillian's dismay, I chose not to let it go as a joke, but took it as an opening for a lecture on art and imitation. (It was, after all, a long line.) I told her it was precisely because this was the real thing that people traveled from all over the world to see it. It's because we know that this is the one Michelangelo himself conceived of, I said, this is the one he sweated over, the one he touched with his very own hands. What we were about to see was not a cheap knockoff by some shortcut artist with no vision of his own.

When we finally got inside the gallery and stood in front of *David,* I could tell that Gillian was impressed. And I suspect that it had little to do with my extemporaneous lecture but was the sheer majesty of Michelangelo's work. His idealization of humanity succeeds for us, regardless of age, race, color, creed, or sex. He is an idealization of ourselves, and that's what artists do best for us.

As I'd feared, even the treasure trove of Italian art had a limited hold on the teenage attention span. When we got to the Uffizi Gallery, Gillian decided to lead us on an express tour through all forty-four rooms, pausing long enough only to note any and all paintings with horses in them. Then she rushed us over the bones of Michelangelo, Rossini, Machiavelli, et al., buried beneath the floor of Santa Croce, slowing the pace down only long enough to admire the teenage boys playing soccer in the square in front of the church. She was definitely showing her age, as attested to by her journal:

MARCH 30
I've heard of overdosing on many things, but never too much culture.

We've been to so many churches, museums, towers, historical places, burial grounds. I can't even count that high. I won't be surprised if I have nightmares tonight about all the paintings and sculptures. They are beautiful, but there is not enough time to look at everything. When you walk into a room and the whole thing is covered with paintings, you are overwhelmed. A person can only absorb so much "stuff" in one day.

I miss my horse!

At first, leaving Florence in the rain seemed a happy circumstance. It was no mere decorative rain, like the one that fell on the roof of our château in St-Rémy, but since this was to be our heaviest driving day, it seemed better to have rain on the roof of the car than on our heads as we toured a town. We were on our way to Menton, just over the French border, with — *Mama mia!* — a stopover in Genoa restored to our itinerary. We had convinced ourselves that we could not leave Italy without some genuine Genovese pesto. History and culture were not all I would be force-feeding Gillian.

With all the demythologizing that has gone on in America in the past forty years, the one piece of American folklore that seems evergreen at home is that we are the freest people on earth. It is a belief, however, that does not transplant well to Western Europe. This was quickly evident to Gillian who, after our second night in Barcelona, wrote in her journal, "The difference between our country and this one is phenomenal. We are so uptight about so many things that the Europeans could care less about."

What had inspired that observation was a walk down the Ramblas and a cursory glance at the cornucopia of flesh publications available at the magazine kiosks. No brown wrappers, no selected racks behind or under cash registers, no posted warnings to eighteen-year-olds to keep their hands off or risk losing them. Just free and open exhibitions of titillation, seduction, and unabashed, socially unredeeming prurience.

Gillian was right. The Europeans are less uptight than we are, and not just about sex. They appear to have a decidedly laissez-faire attitude about the air they breathe — both indoors and out. "No smoking" sections did not exist in any of the restaurants we entered, and the air in the larger cities made Los Angeles air, the presumed epitome of polluted air, seem positively pristine by comparison.

But the most indulgent European exercise in unfettered freedom is on their roads. Compared to Europe, America, land of the open road, is but a network of conveyer belts. In Spain, France, and Italy, street signs, traffic lights, police — all vestiges of state authority, in fact — appear to give way to the individual's inalienable right to blinding speed. Even the supremacy of Mother Nature is tested by the kilometer crunchers. While we cautiously negotiated the rain-slick autostrada on our way to Genoa, Europeans whizzed by us at speeds that would have defied common sense on a sun-dried highway. Alas, when we emerged from a tunnel outside Viareggio, Mother Nature asserted herself as only she can. She threw a hailstorm at them — and us, the innocent bystanders — and we were suddenly faced with a downhill stretch of icy white treachery. Two cars had already collided

and been scrambled together as a roadblock a hundred yards
ahead of us. Lorna screamed to the girls reclining in the back
of our station wagon to hold on tight while I pumped the
brakes.

One of the two cars had been spun around and faced us
head-on. We fishtailed downhill and came to a miraculous
stop no more than five feet away. The family in that car —
four adults and a very small child — frantically tried to free
themselves before more cars erupted from the tunnel. I was
inclined to follow their lead, but Lorna quickly recalled the
lesson we had learned from the young American who had
encouraged us to go to Florence. His own journey a month
earlier had been interrupted by a twenty-car pileup in the fog.

"Was anyone killed?" Lorna, presciently, had asked him.

"Only those who tried to get out of their cars," he replied.

Lorna compressed his message into two simple English
words. "Stay put!" she shouted. "Stay put!"

But as I looked out our rear window and watched as first a
car and then a van came barreling down the hill toward us . . .
towards Meagan and Gillian first, I was seized by a need to
scoop them up in my arms and run us all out of there. In
an instant, with twenty years of loving and nurturing Meagan
to adulthood, in nine months of sweating over every single
movement in Gillian's life, everything that meant anything to
all of us was coming down to one, fully crystallized decision:
stay put or run.

The first impact was a mere bumper-car jolt, an amusement
park ride without the amusement. The van and car had effectively absorbed each other's momentum before grazing us,
and when we looked back up the hill, two other cars had spun
off into the far lane. Then a black Mercedes rolled out of the
tunnel, and for brief seconds it seemed as if we were all props

in a Daimler-Benz commercial as the stately vehicle came to a perfect stop — in its own tracks.

But we were still stuck in our car, and the miracles were ticking off the meter when another Mercedes, this one a streak of white, shot through the tunnel like a giant cue ball aiming to rearrange our randomly ordered tableau of luck, if not our very lives. He hit the black Mercedes, driving it across the road into the two cars in the far lane, one of which then ricocheted off the guard rail, plowed into the van and car tangled behind us, and pushed the van into us again. It was hard enough this time to elicit screams, prayers, and curses, but fortunately no injuries. We caught our breaths one last time as a big rig peeked its cab out of the tunnel. Either the flashing of brake lights back through the tunnel or all those hours we'd spent in the churches of Florence spared us from further danger as all the traffic finally came to a halt.

As we waited for the police and highway crews to clean up the mess, we consoled one another, took pictures of the pileup, and gave thanks that both we and our car were still functional. I studied the driver of the white Mercedes as he stalked impatiently around the accident scene in his luxuriant topcoat and arrogance. I hated him, perhaps unfairly, but of all the people who came through that tunnel, his reckless speed marked him as the most selfish, the one most willing to sacrifice my life and the life of my family to his own petty destiny. Surely he is not a creature exclusive to the European roadway system. I see plenty like him in my daily commute through Los Angeles — and not all of them are in luxury cars. They drive junks and trucks and bikes, and some even drive practical, mid-size cars. But they're all alike in their single-minded devotion to their own, selfish desires. I realized that in a society where individualism was totally triumphant, they would fill the lives of the rest of us with misery — and danger.

Eventually the injured were put into ambulances, the damaged cars onto tow trucks, and the rest of us headed for the police station in Viareggio. Until then, I'd had no use for my paltry Italian, since everyone with whom we'd dealt spoke perfectly good English. So Gillian, who'd barely mastered *buon giorno* and counting to ten before we left, was not greatly motivated to learn more. At the police station, however, no one spoke any English, and my facility for ordering rooms and dinners in Italian was useless in describing a nine-car pileup. The police, though, were both professional and patient, and soon we were on our way. Our car was dented, and we'd lost the time for taking pesto in Genoa, but the rest of the road was sunny and clear.

In Menton we were greeted by a hotel owner who had perfected her English on yearly visits to her children in the United States. She was the perfect hostess for the end of that day, exuding a grandmotherly concern for our health and well-being that brought to mind that Tennessee Williams line about the kindness of strangers.

A peculiar giddiness underscored our conversation on that and the succeeding days. We had come close to a massive family tragedy and survived. The road back to Barcelona, through Cannes, Toulon, Arles, and Perpignan, was lightened considerably by a newfound joy in the girls' expression. They videotaped each other in all manner of goofiness — and Lorna and me whenever we verged on seriousness. They made up silly songs, like "Wendy, the Snail of the Highway," which may have been about my renewed affinity for the slow lane. And they played movie trivia, giving Lorna and me a short lesson on what films would be the classics of their generation:

The line? "Automobile! Big splash! Lake."
The movie? *Sixteen Candles.*

I would be deliriously happy if, years from now, Gillian could remember that the Baptistery doors are in Florence or that Van Gogh painted *Starry Night* in Arles. If, however, all she can recall of our trip to Europe was that we had endured a rough start in Barcelona to savor a truly memorable night in St-Rémy; or that, as we added our family to a Sunday morning parade of families in Santa Margherita, she had affectionately linked her arm in mine and filled me with an unfathomable happiness; or that we had faced death together in Viareggio only to be reborn into the sublime pleasure of each other's company in Menton — if this is all she ever remembers, then our field trip will live forever as a resounding success.

✎ 9 ✎

THE FOURTH QUARTER

WHEN WE RETURNED from Europe, we learned there would be no room for Gillian at Thacher. My feelings were mixed. On the one hand, I was relieved not to have to come up with that enormous tuition. On the other, I truly believed that Thacher would have given Gillian the best possible opportunity to build on what we'd accomplished and fully realize her academic potential.

Gillian's own feelings were recorded in her journal. "I am a little depressed about not going to Thacher," she wrote, "but I knew it was too good to be true."

Perversely enough, I was gratified by her depression. After the intensity of the past months over her endangered friendships and separation from her old school, Gillian had made an emotional commitment to a school an hour away, a boarding school that would have limited her contact with her friends to occasional weekends. She had been able to make that commitment because she was beginning to see herself in the future; she was maturing. And the idea that she found a school "too good to be true" actually thrilled me. Not a horse, not a boy, not a new outfit from the mall, but a school had been idealized in her mind.

A week later, we read that Thacher's headmaster was resigning under charges of sexual harassment and that three students were being expelled for involvement with drugs. I report this here, not to proclaim that the grapes were sour anyway, but because it points out the truth of Gillian's observation — Thacher was too good to be true. I had been the one to describe it as a paradise, but I knew better. Not Thacher, not Redwood, not the Dan Riley School for a Girl are paradises. Human institutions come with human frailties built-in. The point of the institution is to minimize the damage our frailties can do to us while maximizing the chances for advancing our better selves. As I explained to Gillian, the news from Thacher was not that sex and drugs were rampant, but that standards of behavior were in place and being applied.

It was important for her to hear that. I didn't want that double-barreled article to blast a hole in her confidence in people, their institutions, or her own powers of perception. If the whole Thacher experience turned out to be an exercise in disillusionment, it would have been worse than a waste of time. Why should she ever aim for anything higher if it all might turn to dirt in the end? It helped that Thacher was in the news a week later in a story that showed that human virtue still flowered there. One of its students, calling upon his better self, saved the life of a drowning child who'd become stuck in a drainpipe.

I'd had a brush with heroism myself once. I was nine at the time and on my way home from the library one winter night when I came upon an old woman who had slipped on a patch of ice. She was lying in a pile of snow, crying, cold, and hurt. I told her everything would be all right and ran for help. It had been more a case of good timing than heroism, but the adults around me treated me like a hero, and I never lacked for self-esteem after that.

My father, on the other hand, had woefully little self-esteem. In fact, whenever I would ask him for advice or guidance, he would always say, "Do what you want. You're doing a better job with your life than I've done with mine." It was hard to argue with his logic. While he regularly disappointed or embarrassed me with his financial irresponsibility or his weekend drunks, I was working overtime, piling up good grades and winning student offices, honors, and scholarships; I was always dedicated to making him proud of me. When I became a father myself, working overtime so that my own children could be proud of me, I found it painfully ironic that I was still enduring disappointment and embarrassment — only now from my own children. Whether I was standing beside Meagan in traffic court or listening to teachers tell me that Gillian was working below her potential, I couldn't help but wonder what I was doing there. How was it that my father, who was not far removed from adolescence for most of his life, managed to sit back and bask in the glories of my accomplishments while I, with a master's degree in the study of adolescence, was in a constant scramble to understand and adjust to the vagaries of my children's lives?

Could it have been that my father's laissez-faire attitude was the secret of his success in raising me? What a paradox. He never could have raised me like that if he'd thought more of himself, and having been raised like that, I thought too much of myself to raise my own kids that way.

After she had outgrown adolescence herself, Meagan made two telling comments that I've mined for meaning ever since. The first was that at one point in her teen years, she felt like a failure every time she entered the house of her parents, whom she viewed as high achievers whose accomplishments she could never match. The second was that without our constant prodding and example, she would have settled for much less of herself. They are, of course, perfectly contradictory observations, but the truth of one does not negate the truth of the other. In raising Gillian, I've taken the first observation as a caution and the second as a confirmation for my most dearly held belief about child rearing.

This belief was formalized when I was in college studying adolescents (a decidedly easier task than raising them) and read Erik Erikson's *Identity: Youth and Crisis*. There Erikson observes:

> In looking at the youth of today, one is apt to forget that identity formation, while being "critical" in youth, is really a generational issue. So one must not overlook what appears to be a certain abrogation of responsibility on the part of the older generation in providing those forceful ideals which must antecede identity formation in the next generation — if only so that youth can rebel against a well-defined set of older values.

That was an invaluable piece of advice for me at the time, barely out of my own identity formation stage, and it probably saved me from succumbing to such fuzzy sixties' notions about child rearing as not naming your children so they could retain the dubious right to name themselves. Erikson made enough sense to me so that I could face the challenge of raising children without feeling encumbered by my own value system. I was happy to think that my values, however flawed, would provide both Meagan and Gillian with a standard to measure up to — and possibly rebel against. My own — and to a large degree, Lorna's — philosophical tendencies might at times have created the impression that we, too, were guilty of abrogating that responsibility. After all, we had raised them both in what I called a religiously neutral environment. And politically we gravitated toward the center.

Yet we were both confident that we stood for certain values and ideals and were anxious to know whether we were communicating them clearly enough to Gillian for her to use in her own identity formation. From the beginning, the home school had been less about academic progress than identity formation — which is, I think, the most important business of youth. As eager as I was in that fourth quarter to expand and deepen our studies in various academic areas, the more pressing agenda, only partially hidden from myself, was to continue to examine — and influence, if possible, one last time — Gillian's value system.

In *The Closing of the American Mind,* Allan Bloom demonized Mick Jagger as the dark force behind a worldwide lurch toward anti-intellectualism by the young. Jagger's own lyric, "It's only rock 'n' roll," pretty much sums up the defense against such a charge. Rock/pop/rap is essentially dance music. However, to argue that it's nothing more is disingenuous in the extreme, and those of us who were raised on rock know it. Our dirty little secret is that our parents, teachers, clergy, and politicians were absolutely right to fear the music — it did subvert authority and was sexually liberating. Knowing what we knew about it then and knowing that we created it compounds our responsibility in passing it on to our children.

I'd always been pleased that Gillian had rather broad musical tastes for a teenager. She moved freely between musical styles and eras, stopping long enough (on blessed occasions) to play nothing but the Beatles, for instance, for a week or more. In early spring, however, it was not the Beatles or even

Madonna I caught emanating from Gillian's room but the disturbing sounds of rap.

As a child of rock 'n' roll's first generation, I've always been amazed at each succeeding generation's ability to discover a popular music sound to test the tolerance of previous generations. Rap has been the severest test yet of my own tolerance. I should have taken its arrival in our house as part of Gillian's musical exploration, but I viewed it more as a vermin infestation. For instance, a line from one of the songs Gillian was playing went, "If you like to fuck it, pull that bitch's guts right out."

I am sensitive to the unfairness of indicting an entire musical form or even a song on the basis of one line. As I have done with other outside works that played a part in our curriculum, such as "Heart of the Matter," I tried to secure the rights to reproduce more of the lyrics here to illustrate the overall vileness of the song containing that line, but the company that controls the rights refused permission, sadly demonstrating that those eager to profit by free expression are not necessarily willing to share it — nor even abide by it for others.

I simply wanted those lyrics for the purpose of illustration here. I wasn't about to mount a campaign against rap, knowing full well the pitfalls of that route. Adult attacks on groups or songs invariably heighten teen interest and admiration for those targeted. The fact that 2 Live Crew, the nastiest of the early rap groups (or, in another medium, the TV series *Married . . . with Children*) slithered up from the justly deserved swamp of obscurity on a mere twig of public protest graphically demonstrates how easily good intentions can backfire.

In fact, Gillian herself was oblivious of the song until I called attention to it. She had borrowed the CD that contains it for two significantly milder songs. Nonetheless, with the home school in session, I seized on the issue of rap to pursue a discussion about pop culture.

We began by listening to an adequately offensive rap song together. Gillian was quick to point out that this particular rap about a guy's abusive treatment of "his" woman, variously referred to as "bitch" and "ho," was not true of all rap, that a lot of rap dealt with the difficulties of growing up surrounded by drugs and violence. I agreed. I knew enough about rap to know that some positive messages and powerful descriptions came through it about a life that a white suburban girl like Gillian would otherwise never experience. But I wanted to talk about the language used to convey the messages, both the good and the bad, so I asked her what she thought about the increasing vulgarization of our culture.

She said she didn't know what I was talking about, prompting me to ask myself: If someone yells an obscenity in the middle of a forest and there's no one to hear it or care, is it still an obscenity? It then occurred to me that perhaps I was alone in experiencing that uneasiness between Gillian and myself during our earlier viewing of *Boyz N the Hood*. Perhaps the source of that uneasiness was not what was being said but what was being heard. For Gillian's generation, vulgar language is commonplace in our movies — written, as they often are, by people who believe that is how people speak in real life, because their own experiences are limited to movies in which people speak like that because they are written by people who believe that's how people speak in real life. If Gillian had been watching that film with a peer, they may not have experienced the language as I did.

I asked Gillian if she thought that was so; she said it probably was. I asked if she ever thought language got out of hand. She said that it sometimes did with her friends, that often after extended periods of loose talk, they would check their use of vulgarity. "The boys especially get on the girls about it," she said. "They use it all the time themselves, but every once in while they tell the girls to stop talking like that. But it's not just bad language," she added. "Sometimes you use something like 'love' too much. Like everyone's talking about how much they 'love' somebody or something. Like 'I love him' or 'I love this about that person,' and you're using it all the time and everyone knows it's not really love, so you change and start using 'like' instead."

I deemed it a helpful insight into the current generation's attitude toward language, and I tried to return the favor by showing how a previous generation may have laid the groundwork for that attitude. I put an old sixties song on the turntable, "We Can Be Together," a scathing political protest by the Jefferson Airplane. I told Gillian it had broken a language barrier of sorts itself when it was released. But that barrier seemed to be lost on Gillian on her first listening. I was betrayed by the technology. Digital sound has made listening easy for Gillian's generation, so although they may not hear what adults hear in music, they don't miss a word. My recording of "We Can Be Together" was on vinyl, with all the scratches accumulated over twenty years. Even I had trouble deciphering the breakthrough lyric. It served to remind me of an even earlier controversial lyric, the legendary "Louie Louie," which had me and my eighth-grade classmates playing it endlessly in search of the racy lyric that tantalized the teenage underground of our time.

There was no help either on the lyric sheet that accompanied "We Can Be Together," and therein lay the most graphic example of this vulgarization process. The printed sheet contained the line:

Up against the wall fred.

It seems such a quaint dodge in retrospect. What the Jefferson Airplane was actually singing was:

Up against the wall, motherfuckers.

What had happened to our society in twenty or so years, I asked Gillian, so that it was now unnecessary to camouflage such lyrics, and was the change for the better or worse?

She said it was for the better. "If that's what they're singing, that's what they're singing," she said. "What's fred got to do with it?"

She hadn't a clue about how things got to this point, but she gave me a look that said she knew I had one. I did, and it came from one of my most memorable classroom experiences.

It was 1971, my first year of teaching; the class was called Rock as Poetry, and I had just handed out the lyrics to two Jefferson Airplane songs. One was a lovely romantic ballad called "Comin' Back to Me"; the other was "We Can Be Together." The object of the lesson was simple: how one group used tone and language to convey two entirely different messages. The lesson got complicated, however, when the school principal entered the class unannounced to make his first formal observation of my teaching.

I explained my options to Gillian: (1) spend the whole period discussing the merits of "Comin' Back to Me"; (2) discuss the sanitized lyric sheet of "We Can Be Together" and forget about playing the song itself, (3) abandon the lesson altogether and give the students a bogus writing assignment for the day. Because I was young, idealistic, and bold, I went ahead with the lesson as planned. Ears were better then, and when the sorrowful school stereo emitted "Up against the wall motherfuckers," there was a gasp in the room. By the second refrain, the tension was palpable, and it remained so through our discussion of the social and political conditions that led the Jefferson Airplane to write such an angry song.

The next day I met with the principal to discuss my class. There was a time, he said, when he would have had my job for that class, but he recognized that times had changed. And he saw that I had a serious purpose in the lesson and that I had conducted the lesson in a worthy, professional manner. He told me to keep up the good work.

As I told Gillian, I left his office with two impressions: one was that I was working for the right guy — and grateful for it; the other was that words really were very powerful.

That second impression led to one of the most effective lessons I ever taught at the school, which I called the Most Powerful Word in the English Language. I talked to the class (and to many classes after that) about the power of words — taboo words. We discussed how the mere utterance of certain words could cause the kind of tension that had been created in the classroom that day, how such an utterance could have caused me to lose my job or might even cause a presidential candidate to lose an election. As I had done with my students in 1971, I took out my copy of Sir James Frazer's *New Golden Bough* and read to Gillian about the Galla kingdom of Ghera, where taboo words could cost lives:

> . . . the birth name of the sovereign may not be pronounced by a subject under pain of death, and common words which resemble it are changed for others. Thus when a queen named Carre ruled over the kingdom, the word hara, which means smoke, was exchanged for unno; further, arre,

"ass," was replaced by culula; and gudare, "potato," was dropped and loccio substituted for it.

Like my students before her, Gillian reacted strongly to the idea of someone's facing execution for simply saying a word like potato. "That's so stupid," she said. It had struck me as stupid, too, back then — stupid and totally irrational. A primitive society could be excused for such superstitions; a civilized society, however, where grown men and women quaked at the sight or sound of four-letter words was not so easily understood.

That was the essence of the argument that drove the loosely confederated language liberation movement of the sixties, and I confessed to Gillian that I had become part of it. Inspired by General Lenny Bruce and led by Field Commander George Carlin, our objective was to drive irrationality and superstition out of the English language. We succeeded beyond our wildest dreams. There is not now a word in American English that is too taboo for mass consumption. I cannot be shocked, then, when my children are not shocked by what used to be regarded as shocking language. That was the intent then, and I have to live with the irony that my generation, the Baby Boom generation, may, in fact, be the last generation of Americans who, to paraphrase Mark Twain, blushes . . . or needs to.

Having, in effect, owned up to my complicity in creating a society in which something as foul as the rap lyric quoted above could be retailed as entertainment for children, I had to be careful not to seem like a raging hypocrite in discussing it with Gillian. Some people, of course, would find it unconscionable that I would even allow the vain notion of my own hypocrisy to be weighed against my clear responsibility as a parent here. Better to be a hypocrite, they would argue, than allow a young girl to have continued exposure to such aural toxicity. But I believed then, and still do, that outright censorship is not the best way of handling these matters.

I think it's essential to our democracy that the U.S. Constitution prevents sometimes wild-eyed fathers of fourteen-year-olds such as myself from breaking down the doors of Congress to demand that the First Amendment be changed to save our daughters from the excesses of rock or rap or *Three's Company*. It would be so much easier, of course, if we could just walk into our children's rooms, confiscate all offensive media, and announce that three fourths of the States had ratified a new amendment to the Constitution making it illegal to watch, read, or listen to it. The frustration of our system is that it doesn't allow that; the beauty of it is that it leaves it up to us as individuals to deal with the situation in our own homes in our own ways.

One of those ways may, in fact, be censorship. The family home is not the U.S. House of Representatives, and I think parents have an inalienable right to abridge their minor children's freedom of expression whenever they deem it necessary. And I've done so myself. In her senior year of high school, Meagan dressed for school one morning in a sweatshirt with the name of a popular beer emblazoned across the front. I told her she could not wear it to school. For me, spending money so our children can serve as walking billboards for large corporations is one of those vulgarities that too often goes unnoticed. But my objection to letting Meagan wear that sweatshirt that morning was because it promoted beer drinking, a clearly established danger to the lives of teenagers.

I could have been equally censorious with Gillian's rap CD. And I did do some abridging of free expression. By the end of our discussion, I had established some ground rules for playing rap at home: she had to control the volume so that I did not have to hear it; I didn't want any guests to ever hear it; and I didn't want our neighbors to hear it. The overall objective of the Dan Riley School for a Girl, however, was to provide enlightenment, not censorship. From the outset my aim had been to burden Gillian with thought.

During our discussion, I had asked her what might be the bounds of free expression in twenty years when she might have children of her own. But Gillian, who wisely steers clear of hypothetical questions, refused to speculate. And when I asked her how she would react if she walked into the bedroom of a youngster of her own and found her listening to a song that encouraged, say, animal mutilation, she again refused to offer an opinion. Fortunately, I had come to recognize when things were registering with Gillian. In lieu of nicely articulated responses, she sometimes just left me with one of two basic looks. One said: OK, let's get on with this. The other said: I hadn't thought about that before, but I will now. Happily, in this case I was clearly getting the latter look.

Much in the media may be mindless, but I'd determined that my kids would not consume it mindlessly. There is too much in our culture that's violent and vulgar for a parent to be running around everywhere trying to turn off everything objectionable. As with TV, I thought it better to turn Gillian into a discriminating consumer and hope that in helping her develop a sensibility for pop culture, she would become more discerning about much else. The debasement of our language has not been limited to music, movies, and TV. I hoped that Gillian would become sensitive, as well, to the offense committed when an employer describes a massive layoff as a "work force imbalance correction," or a politician tries to explain away a lie as "misspeaking," or the Pentagon camouflages killing the wrong people under euphemisms like "friendly fire."

Gillian, I felt, was already off to a good start in this direction with her earlier question, "What's fred got to do with it?"

Almost every day during the home school year, I passed a young girl on the Pacific Coast Highway waving placards at homebound commuters. Her publicly proclaimed beliefs were inscribed in crayon on posterboard and read like a giant deck of flash cards for liberal causes. One day it was CUT OFF AID FOR EL SALVADOR; another it was NO BLOOD FOR OIL; then it was LEGALIZE ABORTION NOW; then END THE DEATH PENALTY. Some days, I felt genuine affection for the girl, either out of sympathy with her cause du jour or the loneliness of her vigil. Other days, she struck me as a bit of a "Doonesbury" character, so comically earnest and ineffectual. But most of the time I just marveled at the upbringing she must have had to sacrifice hours of watching sitcoms or listening to rap in order to devoutly parade her political convictions. I wondered what it took to raise a child with such dedication, and I wondered whether, if I'd known the answer, I would have applied it to my own children. Would it have been part of our curriculum, with the goal of getting Gillian out on the streets with her own signs of protest?

Gillian had one early flirtation with political activism. One of her encounters with school authorities in the seventh grade stood out from all the rest. At the start of the Gulf War, some of the students had asked the school administration to allow them to have a "Support Our Troops" rally. The administration refused, so a handful of students decided to hold an unsanctioned rally. Gillian was among those who walked out between classes, hoping by their boldness to inspire the other students to join them. The other students did not, and a mild reprimand followed for those who had walked.

If there's any such thing as an inevitable irony, this would be it: Gillian, a daughter of Vietnam War protesters (as Lorna and I had been), engaging in a pro-war demonstration. Odd or not as ironies go, it was peripheral to the larger dilemma Gillian's action had presented. On the one hand, what she had done was of a piece with most of her behavior throughout the year: she had once again chosen to defy school authority. On the other hand, she had done so in the great American tradition of citizen protest, sanctioned by both her school and her parents.

Gillian sensed a difference between the "trouble" she had gotten into that day and her prior run-ins with school authorities: whereas in the latter case we always heard about her infractions from the school, in this case she immediately told us what had happened herself. And her telling left me perplexed. I frankly doubted the depth of her feelings on the Gulf War since she did not really follow the news in those days. I suspected that her motivation for taking part had less to do with showing support for the troops and more to do with withholding support for school authority. Yet I wanted to validate both her forthrightness in telling us about the incident and the principle of free assembly. So we dispensed with the usual lecture on the need to conform to school rules and discussed instead — without advocacy — the pros and cons of the Gulf War and the exercise of First Amendment rights.

That process of neutralizing an issue and examining the underlying values or principles became an integral part of the home schooling effort. I had realized that one of the difficulties in teaching values in school, even a home school, is that they are often confused with issues or must be clarified through them, and issues are more often than not political and therefore divisive. So although it's often easy for people to agree on values (for instance, the value of human life) they often can't agree on issues that turn on those values (abortion or capital punishment).

I'd seen enough of abortion rights rallies, both for and against, where children were trotted out as props by their parents, to know that I never wanted Gillian to become a little soldier in the armies of the righteous, who reduce political convictions to handmade posters and political dialogue to screaming in the face of their opponents. I continually sought to take her to what I perceived to be the vital, open territory between knee-jerk orthodoxy and jerk-off apathy. That territory, I believed, was where the kind of thinking takes place that develops strong convictions and the persuasive tools necessary to convert others to your cause.

On April 23, the State of California executed Robert Alton Harris, the first exercise of capital punishment in the state in twenty-five years. It was nostalgia time for me. When I was Gillian's age, the capital punishment debate swirled around Caryl Chessman; and my first school debate was on the question of whether Chessman should live or die.

The Harris case was Gillian's introduction to the issue. And it was just the kind of case to keep the debate alive until Gillian's own children have to face it. Harris's crime was unquestionably heinous — the cold-blooded killing of two high school boys whose car he wanted for a robbery. Harris had a predictably exculpating background: the child of an alcoholic mother and an abusive father, abandoned by both at the age of fourteen. When I saw a picture of Harris as a smiling eight-year-old, I couldn't help but think of the effort I'd put in with Gillian over the past nine months, chasing all the way back to the womb to understand why she wasn't doing better in school. There are little Robert Alton Harrises all over the place, growing up with no one caring anything at all about them, least of all whether they live or die — until, that is, they kill someone.

Gillian reacted to the story in a very human way. If the murdered boys had been her friends, she said, or if Harris had murdered anyone in her family, she'd want him executed right away. We turned to that Don Henley song again:

> The more I know, the less I understand
> All the things I thought I knew, I'm learning again
> I've been trying to get down to the heart of the matter
> But my will gets weak and my thoughts seem to scatter
> But I think it's about forgiveness
> Forgiveness.

Gillian got the point immediately. Earlier, we had agreed on the power of forgiveness — its necessity; its value as the key organizing principle of our lives. Without it, animosities harden and become intractable; cooperation and progress between people end. Without it, Gillian and I might still be lost on that dark, winding road — each alone. At the end of "Heart of the Matter," however, she nodded her head in sober recognition of this added dimension to the whole notion of forgiveness. It was one thing to practice it between father and daughter, or mother and daughter, between siblings, friends, or acquaintances, but to be truly meaningful as a basic value, forgiveness had to be extended to moral aliens like Robert Alton Harris.

Despite the vagueness of her religious upbringing, Gillian had always described herself as a Christian. We had in the past superficially discussed that identity in terms of certain holidays. Then, of course, we had gotten into it more deeply in the second quarter of the home schooling in terms of myth, literature, film, and music. The case of Robert Alton Harris, however, provided Gillian with her first opportunity to confront the deeper moral implications of being a Christian. She was welcome to assume a full Christian identity if she wanted — with my blessing, for what that was worth. But I didn't want her being conned by those dedicated to diluting or perverting the meaning of that identity. Her initial reaction to the Harris case had been the very human one of revenge. Genuine Christian living, however, with forgiveness at its core, would demand more of her than that.

Three days after Harris's execution, an article appeared in the *L.A. Times* in the lower right-hand corner of the paper — "below the fold," in newspaper parlance — far beneath the lofty reaches of space reserved for the killers of children. The headline read:

> RELICS OF BIG BANG SEEN FOR 1ST TIME;
> COSMOS: RESEARCH CONFIRMS THAT
> EXPLOSION STARTED THE UNIVERSE

The thrust of the article was that science had basically discovered the origin of the universe. "For the first time," the paper reported, "scientists have observed long-sought relics of the 'Big Bang,' the controversial theory that the universe was created by a primeval explosion 5 billion years ago."

It seemed like a major story to me. In fact one scientist quoted called it "one of the major stories of the century." Another said, "If you're religious, it's like looking at God." Given the position of the story, however, it would be hard to convince Gillian of its significance. Early on, we'd had a lesson on the layout of a newspaper and how the positioning of articles reflected what the editors valued as important. On the day this article appeared, more prominently placed stories included: RAPES VASTLY UNDERCOUNTED, STUDY CONCLUDES and SKY DIVERS KILLED IN CRASH DID NOT WEAR SEATBELTS.

For three days before this story, the saga of Robert Alton Harris had received banner headlines. In the end the nagging question came down to: is KILLER EXECUTED so much bigger a story than SCIENTISTS SEE FACE OF GOD?

It was another way of asking a question I'd wanted Gillian to consider throughout the home school: Did the media reflect society's values or did it shape them? In my own consideration of the question, I was reminded of the response in the early seventies when Walter Cronkite was asked why the media dwelt on the negative all the time. He said something to the effect that reporting on how many cats didn't get lost in a day was not news — the cat that did get lost was the news. I think he was right then. But to my seemingly endless list of worries, I could add that Gillian, it appeared, was now growing up in a world where all the cats in the neighborhood *were* getting lost or beaten, drowned, run over by trucks, or eaten by dogs. The really big news now was the cat that survived — or, less metaphorically, the politician who kept his word, the banker who did right by her depositors, the defense contractor who avoided cost overruns, the cop who went by the book, the lawyer who upheld the spirit of the law as well its letter, and so on.

In the *Living Planet* series, we had come upon a description of cichlids, fish that hide their young in their mouths to protect them from danger even after hatching. As we studied them, Gillian was moved to remind me, "Remember, Dad, we're not cichlids." I tried to keep that in mind. Occasionally, like most parents, I'd like to be a cichlid, spitting Gillian out to swim on her own only when I was sure the coast was clear. But nature made humans otherwise, and I'd always felt that the best way to protect my own young from danger was to keep them focused on what are commonly referred to as life's realities.

Yet, as the home schooling year progressed and I saw the world's news in terms of how it must look to the young, I began to wonder about our concept of reality. It seemed that it was increasingly becoming one-sided — the dark side. Murderers, rapists, crash victims — lost cats all — are taken as real. The cosmos is mere diversion. Reality, like the language that expresses it in Gillian's world, may now have become similarly polluted. To be taken seriously, to earn placement "above the fold," it seemed, the news must make us wince, make our skin crawl and our stomachs turn, make our hearts heavy and our heads swim, must magnify our common lowliness.

If the *L.A. Times* didn't think the big bang was worth the same amount of time, space, and energy as Robert Alton Harris, I would have to make up for that imbalance. I read one astonishing sentence in the big bang article three times to Gillian alone before calling in her mother and sister to repeat it twice more: "The Big Bang is perhaps one of the most difficult physics concepts for laymen to accept. Its chief assumption is that 5 billion years ago all matter in the universe was compressed into an unimaginably dense sphere smaller than the period at the end of this sentence."

In matters of physics, I am the layman nonpareil. There is little that I can be told in that area that will not either amaze or confound me. And that sentence right there was the single most amazing and confounding sentence I'd ever read or heard in my life. The universe . . . the size of a period at the end of a sentence. I could not help repeating it over and over in hopes of somehow grasping it.

Gillian, on the other hand, took it in stride, as if I had said, When it rains, things get wet. I asked her whether this was not the most amazing and confounding thing she had ever heard in her life, and she said, "Dad, none of these things are as unbelievable to me as they are to you. You tell me about the Soviet Union breaking up and the universe coming out of this little dot, and you think it's so incredible because you always looked at things one way, and now you have to look at them a new way. But for me, I'm just learning this stuff, so it's the only way I've ever seen these things."

Ka-boom again.

It was one of the two or three most enlightening moments for me during our school year, one of those plain-as-the-nose-on-your-face revelations that you never see until someone holds a mirror up to you. Gillian held the mirror up to me so that I could see that she was learning things (including what not to learn) in ways and at a pace that I simply hadn't calculated. I'd been trying to teach her for so long, but I really had no idea what it was like for her to grow up in an era of instant communication, where the pace of change is so fast. The past has been created for her and her generation quicker than they can possibly digest it, and the present is an object of constant sensory bombardment. The past, as a consequence, is neither easily accessible nor credible, and the present is a light show, all imagery and illusion.

The period at the end of the sentence business rang a bell for me, and I thought I'd make one more attempt at amazing and confounding Gillian. I fetched Norman O. Brown's *Love's Body* and immediately found this passage: "Creation

out of nothing. Time and space are integrated into that ultimate pointlike unity, *bindu,* point, dot, zero, drop, germ, seed,
semen. The primal oudad."

I told Gillian it was from a book published in 1966. In that
passage, Brown was referring to two earlier works, and one of
those was centuries-old Tibetan mysticism. I said, "Now you
have to find that amazing. Here are all these scientists running
around proclaiming this great discovery, and some Tibetan
monk probably figured it all out eons ago."

But Gillian just shrugged it off, "Maybe it was in that
Alexandria Library that burned down. Didn't we learn in the
Cosmos series that it was full of stuff that we've just been
learning all over again anyway?"

Ka-boom.

Ka-boom.

Ka-boom.

A week after science had looked into the face of God, all hell
broke loose in the streets of Los Angeles. Once again real
life was intersecting with our studies. We were in the middle of reading *To Kill a Mockingbird* — another father, another time, trying to guide his children through the thicket of
American race relations — when the jury in the first trial of
four white police officers accused of beating Rodney King, a
black motorist stopped for speeding, issued not guilty ver-
dicts.

In her journal Gillian recounted the day this way:

APRIL 29

The verdict came over the radio as I was cleaning Nigel's
feet — Not guilty on the Rodney King beating.

It flew right over my head because at the moment I didn't
remember who Rodney King was. The message was aired

about every ten minutes. When I got home, I must have been asked about 50 times if I had heard — way more than the news about Magic.

After I'd remembered who Rodney King was, I was shocked that they could have found the police innocent.

I found it interesting, and somewhat reassuring, that Gillian would compare the King news to the day a few months earlier when Magic Johnson announced his retirement from basketball because he had the HIV virus. One of my concerns had long been that she was growing up blasé, that events were always flying right over her head because there were so many of them and she was keeping her head down in defense.

If nothing else, Magic's announcement and the King verdict demonstrated that the world — or at least our part of it — had not become totally unshockable. Whether Gillian and her peers would one day be able to recall where they were the day they heard the news about Magic or the King verdict with the same degree of clarity that members of my generation recall where they were when they heard that JFK had been shot remains to be seen. On the surface, the events are not wholly comparable, but the power of certain moments to scar the memory arises from their total unexpectedness. I can't tell yet if Gillian has been scarred by the Magic Johnson and Rodney King stories. I hope so. I hope her whole generation has. In the first instance, personal survival may depend upon it; in the second, our nation's surely does.

In introducing the Civil War segment of his *America* series, Alistair Cooke quoted from Thomas Jefferson's journal words Jefferson had written after watching a planter abuse a slave in front of the planter's small son:

The whole commerce between master and slave is a perpetual exercise of the most boisterous passions, the most unremitting despotism on the one part and degrading submissions on the other. Our children see this and learn to imitate it. . . . The parent storms, the child looks on . . . and puts on the same airs in the circle of smaller slaves. . . . And thus nursed, educated and daily exercised in tyranny, cannot but be stamped by it with odious peculiarities. The man must be a prodigy who can retain his manners and morals undepraved by such circumstances.

Cooke felt compelled to apologize that Jefferson had himself been a slaveholder, as if that devalued his wisdom. It's Jefferson's very standing as a slaveholder, of course, that adds resonance to the words. The slavers, the bigots, the genteelly prejudiced, are the ones who have to recognize that they carry the virus of racial hatred if we're to save ourselves from being further afflicted with it.

I'd found it perplexing that although at home we had constantly stressed the value of education at least as much as racial tolerance, the first constantly needed reinforcing with both girls while the second clearly and firmly took root. I was perplexed but not unhappy. Indifferent study habits, as Meagan had proved, could be outgrown. Bigotry, on the other hand, is like blood disease, and a parent who passes it on to a child ought to be equally alarmed.

On a number of occasions, Gillian had expressed bewilderment over the origins of prejudice. We reread the Jefferson quotation together. Then, to put it in personal perspective, I told her a story from when I was no more than three or four years old. A woman passed by our home who, in the more liberal parts of our town at the time, would have been called colored. She was the first such person I'd ever seen in my life, and as she passed me I pointed up to her and asked a question so cruel that it could only have come from the mouth of a bigot or the mouth of a babe. The question need not be repeated here, but I did repeat it for Gillian's sake. The poor woman passed on in an embarrassed silence, which, I suspect, was an all-too-familiar refuge for her. My mother was the only other person present and the only one with the power to make meaning out of the incident. Had she reacted as I had to Gillian's ghastly spelling in the "gost" story — laughing about it, sharing its "cuteness" with friends and relatives — I may have grown up to be as bad a racist as Gillian is a speller. Instead, my mother, who, by today's loose definition of the word, might be called a racist herself, took me by the hand, marched me into the house, and began to educate me on the differences among people and the importance of being toler-ant of those differences. Her attitude toward racial tolerance, I later realized, was much like her attitude toward education; although she had been limited in both by her own upbringing, she knew that both were essential if her children were to grow up as better people.

Another mother with as clear-eyed a vision of her child's future made her stand right after the L.A. riots. Among the many horrible scenes we had witnessed, one of the most dis-tressing was a photo that appeared in the *Times* of a defiant six-year-old black boy giving the police the finger from the backseat of a car full of older boys as it pulled away from a riot scene. One morning, a month later, Gillian and I read a letter of apology in the paper from Reginald Leroy Gardner II, the boy in the picture. He'd been recognized in the photo by his mother, Davette Demery, a twenty-six-year-old single mother from South-Central Los Angeles, who had left him in the care of relatives the first day of the riots only to learn from the photo that he'd spent it with gang members. In a letter to the *Times,* she expressed her resolve to overcome the obstacles to raising a responsible child in a harsh inner-city environment and her determination to turn the embarrassment of the photo into a life lesson for her son. "I don't believe in flowing with the crowd," she told readers. "I explained that to him and told him if he wanted the best in life he had to work hard for a better lifestyle."

I thought the mother's action was heroic in and of itself. And for those of us reading *To Kill a Mockingbird,* it provided a vivid, contemporary parallel to the story of a parent trying to lift its young from a rat's nest of social antagonisms. Without the benefit of a horse, a trip to Europe, or a forty-five-mile buffer zone between home and the mean streets, it seemed to me that the Davette Demery School for a Boy was now in session in South-Central L.A.

The riot had an impact, not only on our literature studies, but on our history studies as well. We were sent back to reconsider the American Revolution in light of the newly minted theory that the riot was actually a rebellion — the opening shots in a second American Revolution. The underpinning of this theory was the alleged analogy between the Boston Tea Party and the looting of various Los Angeles businesses that provided jobs, goods, and services to the riot-torn area.

I was relieved to find that Gillian's shock at the King verdict wasn't so severe that it shorted out her powers of perception. Her analysis was simple but clearheaded; she wrote:

The aftermath has been horrible. Of course half or maybe more of those people just want an excuse to be violent. By now, everyone's probably forgotten what they were . . . out there for.

Hello, people, trashing your neighborhood, which is already a mess, isn't going to help Rodney King at all.

To make the historical point, I suggested to her that if the Americans of 1776 had burned down the Old North Church, torn up Boston Common, and shot Paul Revere's horse, the L.A. riot as prelude to revolution might have made some sense. But they didn't. They, like my mom in the forties and that mom from South-Central, had their eyes on the future.

Ironically, as the riot raged through Los Angeles, Meagan received her acceptance from New York University's prestigious Tisch School of the Arts. She had taken the last quarter of the school year off to earn some money and go through the arduous application process. Despite our East Coast roots, Lorna and I viewed New York as a city violently out of control, so we had been less than enthusiastic about Meagan's going to NYU. But with the police and citizens of Los Angeles turning roadside beatings into public sport, ethnic groups arming themselves to do battle over shoe outlets and fast-food restaurants, and the fire next time seemingly upon us, our case against New York as the citadel of violence collapsed.

The distance between Los Angeles and Thousand Oaks did provide buffer enough to allow Meagan to celebrate her achievement from the safety of our living room as smoke billowed from the burning city on our TV screen. It was an odd, vaguely uncomfortable juxtaposition of events. But as Meagan danced around, waving her letter of acceptance in the air, I watched Gillian's face transformed from distress at a world in chaos to a mixture of admiration for and wonder at a big sister who'd accomplished something rather difficult by dint of her own very hard work. In the long run, I thought, that might prove to be the most valuable lesson Gillian would learn that year.

The personal interaction between Gillian and myself through the latter part of the fourth quarter was probably the best it had been since she was an infant and we knew nothing but bliss between us. The few flareups — over a math assignment that didn't get finished or dishes that didn't get done on time — were quickly extinguished, as much by her efforts as mine. In the past, Gillian had seemed resigned to an endless series of confrontations; now, in contrast, she became genuinely and actively involved in resolving them, and proved very adept at using humor to do so. At one point I'd left her with a bunch of nasty distance-times-rate-times-time problems and returned to find them unfinished. "I knew how to do them before you left the room," she explained, "but once you were gone, I could feel my brain cells dying. I think we should forget the math and look into this as a science project."

I truly believed we had freed ourselves once and for all from the rat's nest of our own antagonisms. So when we ended up having our very worst confrontation just before school closed for the summer, I was the one in shock. To an extent, it was another bit of fallout from the Rodney King verdict. Gillian was supposed to have gone to a rock concert at the L.A. Sports Arena at the height of the riots. The concert was rescheduled on a later date. Gillian attended, got home late (not beyond her curfew, just late), and woke up the next day in the foul temper that often afflicts people who don't get enough sleep. I knew it well, especially that day, because I was in the same frame of mind owing to an eight-hour writing seminar I was preparing for Lorna's company the following day. As I drove Gillian down to the corral, with both of us pitched deep into our respective bad humors, we had no trouble coming to a quick disagreement on the time she was to come home. I said 4:30; she said 5:30. I insisted; she resisted.

Gillian was supposed to be working on her last big project of the school year — a research paper. We needed time together at the library that evening so that she would have her work for the next day while I was delivering the seminar. She argued that I was not allowing her enough time to do everything she had to do with Nigel. I said that I still had more work to do for the seminar and I needed to get our library business finished on time.

We sat in the car outside the corral facing each other, the shadow of an awful night presumably from another lifetime growing over us. We had become the Bully and the Brat again. I was determined to exercise my parental prerogative, set the time, and stand by it. She was determined to make me stand by it for an hour longer.

I told her she was wasting her valuable time with Nigel by sitting there, arguing. She told me I was exaggerating how much time we would need at the library. I told her I'd been taking students through research projects for ten years and knew more than she did about how much time was needed. She told me I knew nothing about horses, though, and that Nigel needed tending then and there. I told her the argument was getting neither of us anywhere and that I'd be back to pick her up at 4:30.

She got out of the car, slammed the door behind her, and walked away, shouting over her shoulder, "I won't be here 'til 5:30!"

I rolled down my window and shouted back at her, "Four-thirty!"

She disappeared around the corner into the corral.

I returned at 4:30 and parked outside the corral for twenty minutes, then angrily drove home.

In all the confrontations we'd had in the past, Gillian had never crossed the line to outright defiance. She'd evade, she'd avoid, she'd plead ignorance or play the victim, but she'd never crossed that line. Now that she had, I found myself swaying helplessly, sickeningly, between rage and despair. If it had happened nine months earlier, I probably would have taken it as another malignant growth in our progressively degenerating relationship. But its coming near the very end of all this effort to establish communication and trust filled me with a sense of utter failure.

"She's just undone nine months of hard work," I cried to Lorna.

I didn't know how we'd ever salvage the situation — or the year. I didn't know how I was going to get into a proper frame of mind for my seminar the next morning. I didn't know how I'd sleep that night. I couldn't think of a punishment harsh enough to compensate for the damage she had done.

The next morning there was a letter from Gillian on my bathroom mirror. I ripped it off, stuffed it into my briefcase, and hurried off to the seminar. I read it during a morning break. It said:

Dan —

Sometimes I forget. I forget that relationships of any shape, size, color and kind need to be fed. They need to be fed with love and laughter, with tears and fears, joy and pain, give and take, and so on and so on.

I, being the 14-year-old girl that I am, forget . . . forget to take care of my relationships just as well as I would take care of, say, Nigel. I don't always feed them properly. Some are too fat. Some strong. Some are too skinny. And some are weak. When they just get a scratch, a bruise, or sprain an ankle, they heal. When they get hit hard, they die. The strong are hard to kill. The scratches sometimes feel worse, but they are not. And they get better if you don't worry about who scratched who and just feed them a strict diet of love, laughter, joy, and giving.

Sometimes I forget how trusted I am, and how much freedom I have for a 14-year-old. I forget that there are limitations, authorities, and expectations which must not be crossed, must be respected, and must be met.

I am truly sorry for not meeting those today. Everyone steps out of line once in a while. My house that I'm building has the foundation down good, and the first story's up. Once I forgot it was my house and threw rocks at the window. Good thing I remembered it was mine before I broke one.

I wish you the best of luck today on your seminar. Please forgive me. I'm sorry.

Love,
Jillian

So the Dan Riley School for a Girl, which effectively began with a letter, would end with a letter. Whether or not this was as false a letter of contrition as the first was the nasty question that arose out of my still-simmering anger. Had Gillian merely become a more facile, manipulative writer of letters — misspellings and mixed metaphors aside? Or had she become a more thoughtful and honest writer of letters, moved from the heart to undo the damage to a now-valued trust?

In the original instance, of course, I had the much-ballyhooed smoking gun — Gillian standing there amid astonished friends at the teen center dance. There was no such evidence in this case. This was going to have to be a call made from the head — all I'd come to know of Gillian in the past nine months — and from the heart — all I'd come to feel for her.

Almost as an afterthought, I decided to test Gillian's letter on my seminar group. We had just spent the better part of a day talking about how to write effective letters — letters that communicate clearly, solve problems, move relationships and events forward. There in my hand I held a letter that tried to do all those things, and while I was trying to make up my own mind about it, I would offer it and its background to a group of strangers and allow them to pass judgment on it.

When I finished reading the letter, the audience — which had been polite and attentive through my previous hours' long discourse on creating good opening sentences, linking paragraphs, restating main points in conclusion — suddenly became impassioned. They stood up, applauding, wiped tears from their eyes, and shook my hand in congratulations on what an obviously fine job the home school had done with Gillian.

It was, to be sure, a gratifying moment, and it couldn't have come at a better time. But as I accepted thanks from the departing participants, many who shared brief glimpses into their own difficulties in raising teens I was struck by how wrong they were. The Dan Riley School for a Girl had not *done* a fine job with Gillian. There was nothing *done* about it. Gillian had more growing and learning to do. She was, I realized just then, still a work in progress.

Yet I also realized that she had now clearly become more progress than work — and no school could ask any more of its students than that.

AFTER SCHOOL

GILLIAN IS NOT THE ONLY WORK in progress; so is the country she was born into. At the outset I said I didn't think that our educational problems are so much endemic to our public schools as they are symptomatic of broader cultural ills. Chief among those ills is this fragmenting image we're creating of ourselves — for ourselves and for our children. The cult of individualism in this country has created, if not exactly 250 million different visions of who we are as a people, then surely enough to distort and confuse the formation of our national identity — which seems so much at the adolescent stage itself. We've stood John Donne on his head — it's not that no man is an island; every man, woman, and child is an island unto his or her own self.

It's no wonder we've seen discipline collapse, respect for learning decline, planning for the future diminish. We've lost the cohesive force of national purpose, and without it there's no compelling argument for doing anything more than quickly satisfying private or, at best, very parochial wants and needs. It's recess time in America. School's out!

We seem unable to rally to the cause of education unless it is framed in terms of national security or economics. In the late fifties and early sixties, when we last faced a crisis in education (ostensibly because the Soviet Union beat us to outer space with Sputnik), we responded with a generous outlay of student loans that we called National Defense Loans, thus justifying the expenditure as we would new missile development. In the late eighties and nineties, all of the various reforms floating around us are the result of our lagging performance in world markets vis-à-vis Germany and Japan. On the face of it, the causality between poor schools and a poor start in the space race or a poor balance of trade is preposterous. When we beat the Soviets to the moon a decade after Sputnik, it was not because we were doing a better job of teaching science in our public schools. We had decided as a nation that getting to the moon was a national goal worthy of our dollars and energy. We had national purpose. Similarly, our reassertion of ourselves as the preeminent global economic power will not be the result of better math programs in school, but because we have a national desire for economic renewal.

Countless efforts are under way to correct the sad condition of American public education. There are calls for longer school days, longer school years; tougher teacher standards, higher teacher pay; making schools smaller, safer, more specialized. One of the most prominent educational movements at the moment is for school vouchers: the government would issue a tuition credit to parents and allow them to apply it to any school of their choosing. As a parent who eagerly pursued a private education for my daughter, both at home and in a more traditional setting, I should be cheering on the voucher movement, but I don't. I think it does nothing less than signal the loudest, most dramatic retreat from the whole idea of American nationhood. John Kennedy can join Donne in the corner: Ask not what you can do for your country, ask what you can do for yourself.

If we're to issue vouchers for education, next we can issue vouchers for highway improvements and become responsible for our own road maintenance. We can issue vouchers for food and drug inspection and become responsible for testing everything we put in our bodies. We can completely dismiss the idea of providing for a common defense and issue security vouchers for walling in neighborhoods and hiring private armies to protect us. A national identity is a Humpty Dumpty kind of creation, oddly formed, fragile, and precariously positioned on a precipice. The voucher movement would push it over and leave us little hope of ever putting it back together again. Scattered around us would be schools of little evangelicals, little feminists, left-wingers and right-wingers, little Afro-Americans, Italo-Americans, Serbo-Americans, but nowhere schools of little Americans. The proponents of vouchers contend that they would offer children a choice of schools. But the choice is for all Americans, and it's bigger than school choice. It is the choice of whether we want to continue working toward that more perfect union we promised ourselves or whether we want to disband into a collection of small, mutually suspicious tribes.

Voucherism would effectively mark the end of the American struggle to forge a fair and free nation out of the disparate peoples of this earth — in a mythical sense, to reclaim Eden. It would be an admission to ourselves and the rest of the world that we the people cannot do it — cannot operate a school system, let alone a government, of, by, and for the people; cannot rise above petty jealousies and selfish motives to achieve a grander version of ourselves.

Soon Gillian will be part of the American educational system again, and one day Gillian and Meagan may have children who are part of it. I want it to work for them, and I believe it needs to work for the sake of our nationhood. The congressionally initiated effort to create national education standards may be a critical step in providing us with a healthy, vigorous school system. But it will have to avoid the obvious pitfalls. It will have to avoid being held hostage to various interest groups who see public schooling only as a means of advancing their own narrow views of the world. It will also have to avoid turning our schools into agents of some national security or industrial policy.

It will have to focus on the real problems of America's young — not that they rank eleventh in worldwide math competency, but that they are plagued by broken families, drugs, promiscuity, intolerance, violence, and suicide. It will have to focus on fundamental educational goals — not raising SAT scores but raising expectations, enthusiasm, and curiosity. It will have to broaden the mandate for our schools — not merely to turn out competent workers but informed citizens, wise consumers, responsible parents, and good neighbors as well.

This national effort will have to accommodate the volatility of the information age, which rewards the play of the mind rather than its content. And it will have to provide for the main business of childhood, certainly of adolescence, which is the formation of a healthy adult identity.

I'll always be glad I opened the Dan Riley School for a Girl. I offer the preceding pages as guidance for any parent with the time, the energy, and the inclination to try it, but less as a solution to an educational crisis than as a means of getting closer to our children and their perception of the world. I think only in doing that can we understand how critical it is that we reaffirm our sense of national identity and purpose. Seeing the world through our kids' eyes keeps our focus on the future and gives us the courage to make the compromises and sacrifices necessary for our more perfect union.

We should neither be deluded by a false nostalgia for an idyllic America that never was nor so consumed with self-loathing for the faults in our past that we give up. History begins with us. All that really matters is what we do from this point on.

Ironically, in *You Can't Go Home Again,* Thomas Wolfe succeeded in pointing the way home when he wrote:

> I believe that we are lost here in America, but I believe we shall be found. . . .
>
> I think the true discovery of America is before us. I think the true fulfillment of our spirit, of our people, of our mighty and immortal land, is yet to come. I think the true discovery of our own democracy is still before us. And I think all these things are certain as the morning, as inevitable as noon. I think I speak for most . . . living when I say that our America is Here, is Now, and beckons on before us, and that this glorious assurance is not only our hope, but our dream to be accomplished.

Basta!

That's Italian for enough. Enough of the big picture. In the end, the home school has been about little pictures — family snapshots. And I have a few more to share.

One day in Europe we were standing outside our hotel in Arles when a woman walked by trailing an Irish Wolfhound, an animal so large it looked as if it should have had a saddle on its back rather than a leash around its neck. So I would be sure not to miss it (as if anyone could), Gillian took my face in her hands and directed my attention to the four-legged spectacle. "So, Dad, what do you think?" she asked.

I knew exactly where the question was coming from and where it was leading. Gillian, not satisfied with a horse, a rabbit, a fish, and a snail, had long been campaigning for a dog. But Lorna and I had drawn a firm line; dogs, unlike horses, could not be kept at a distance in a neighboring corral. A dog was an in-your-face proposition — in your face, in your yard, in your closets, in the crotch of your pants. Despite Gillian's persistence, we had owned no dogs and had vowed to continue owning no dogs.

"Don't even ask about it," I told her, turning my back on the giant canine invading France.

"So, you've still got your heart stuck on Dalmatians," she said without missing a beat.

It was a good, sharp retort and forced me to laugh in spite of myself. Gillian immediately took my laugh as an opening and on the last leg of our trip begged me to provide her with a list of my objections to a dog. Knowing that to provide her with such a list would be to open negotiations, I resisted. Over French and Spanish ground I resisted. Over open seas I resisted. In flying over the American continent I resisted.

Shortly after our return home, Lorna gave Gillian a book for Easter, *Life's Little Instruction Book*. It is filled with simple suggestions of ways to make life more pleasant for ourselves and those around us. Gillian devoured it along with the chocolate bunnies on Easter morning and came to the breakfast table duly inspired.

"I love this book, Mom," she told Lorna, "and I'm going to try and do everything in it."

Lorna was delighted; I was dangerously preoccupied with the Sunday morning paper.

"If I need help doing any of this — like recording your parents' laughter — will you help me?"

Of course, said Lorna, serving up her favorite dish — positive reinforcement.

"Great!" said Gillian. "Page three says, 'Own a dog.'"

And that's how Lorna came to giving Gillian a list of objections to owning a dog. In military terms the strategy is called divide and conquer; nonetheless Lorna came up with a very impressive list:

1. Lorna's allergies
2. We didn't want to pay for a dog.
3. We didn't want to pay for the upkeep of a dog.
4. We didn't want a dog stinking up the house.
5. We didn't want a dog digging up the yard.
6. We didn't want to have to remind Gillian to clean up after her dog.
7. We didn't want to have to remind Gillian to give her dog a bath.
8. We didn't want to have to remind Gillian to feed her dog.
9. We didn't want to have to worry about boarding a dog when we were away.
10. We didn't want to be stuck with a dog when Gillian went off to college.

Gillian, as I'd feared, wasn't at all discouraged by the list. She took it more seriously than any assignment I'd given her over the course of the year. And in a few weeks she was back with her response and pleading for an audience with both of us to make her case. I overcame my reluctance to be part of the audience because I trusted my inner resolve to say no when all was said and done.

Gillian sat with us at the dining room table, the scene of so many family discussions about the missteps in her life. Only now she was in complete control. She had researched the cost of buying and maintaining a pedigreed dog and was prepared to meet those costs. She said she had $240 saved up for the purchase and would dedicate all her future allowance and earnings to vet bills and food. She said Lorna's allergies would not be affected — nor would our furnishings, nor the general aroma of our house — because this would be an outdoor dog. Then she took us outside and showed us an area that she had roped off for a dog run. We had backyard to spare, she explained. "It will be less grass for you to mow," she told me encouragingly. The run would restrict the dog's movement in the yard and thereby minimize the damage it could do to plants, flowers, and the general landscape, and it would make it easy for her to do the daily cleanup that she assured us would be part of her routine. When we were away, she vowed that she and her dog would be inseparable. She'd stay home from any future trips to Europe or New England or even to Disneyland in order to be with her dog, and when she went away to college, her dog would go too. She offered to put all her promises in writing and swore she'd live by the document for the rest of her life.

I smiled without comment throughout the presentation. Since most of it was directed at me, the hard-liner, Lorna was free to watch from the sidelines, and I could see her eyes twinkling with pride as Gillian deftly employed the tools she had learned at her mother's side.

"Now maybe you can help me make a tough decision," Gillian said to me, shifting gears ever so smoothly. "I don't know yet what kind of dog I want." She reached into a pile of books she had assembled in front of her and handed me the one on top, *Rottweilers*. "You wouldn't ever have to worry about anything happening to me if I had one of those to go around with," she said.

My smile broadened, but I still said nothing.

She handed me the second book from her pile, *Dobermans*.

I laughed out loud. "Gillian," I said, "you're killing your case here. You made a great presentation, but there's no way in the world I'm going to even think about owning one of these things."

"Okay," she said, "you've convinced me. It should be a Dalmatian."

And just like that, I had a book on Dalmatians in my hands. "Look at page thirty-six," she said. "Then look at page forty-two."

She had clearly marked the pages, so I had no trouble finding them. "Do you like the black and white ones or the liver and white ones better?"

Fatefully I answered. "The black and white."

"So do I," she said.

With rottweilers and Dobermans glaring up at me from the discarded books on the table, I found myself actually poring over pages of Dalmatians. Gillian gave me all the time I needed to conjure up images of noble Dalmatians racing off to fight fires and adorable Dalmatians outwitting the evil Cruella De Vil. "You don't have to give me your answer right now," she said kindly. "I can wait a while, but I want you to think about something before you decide." Then she picked up the last book and held it before my eyes — *To Kill a Mockingbird*. "Remember what a terrible thing prejudice is," she said.

It was a breathtaking performance — Gillian at her best. If she'd been a fourteen-year-old son and just shown me she could throw a spiraling football seventy yards downfield, I couldn't have been more impressed. "I won't give you an answer right now," I told her. "I would have . . . and I could . . . but out of respect for the time and creativity you put into your presentation I'm going to think about it."

She leaped up from her seat, shouting, "He's going to think about it! He's going to think about it!"

I was amazed at how deeply I thought about it. For the first time in my adult life I was giving serious thought to owning a dog. I said to myself — and Lorna — if Gillian were a sick child or her life were at risk and she wanted a dog, there wouldn't be a second thought about it. We would own a dog — a rottweiler if she wanted. And she had surely made some compelling arguments. A horse, a rabbit, a fish, and a snail, she said, were hardly companionable pets. And it wasn't as if she were a nine-year-old, suddenly infatuated with the idea of owning dog, she added. She was fourteen, she reminded us, and had wanted a dog for most of her life.

Over the week that we had given ourselves to think about the prospect, Lorna and I had come close to relenting twice. We slept on it each time, and by the time decision day arrived, we had slept on it enough to overcome it. Gillian raised the question when just the two of us were in the kitchen, and I responded as gently as I could. I told her that as much as we appreciated her effort, she would have to wait until she was out on her own to have a dog.

I think she was surprised by the answer, although her face registered only disappointment. She said nothing herself, needing, I believe, all her reserves to absorb the bad news. Once she regained her equilibrium, she quietly walked out of the kitchen and went to her room.

I felt wretched, clinging desperately to the logic of my position. As much as Gillian loved her horse, she still had to be reminded to ride him; she had to be reminded to feed the rabbit and clean the aquarium. A dog would surely be added to the list of things we would have to nag her about. Meagan, our first animal lover, had already abandoned a horse on our doorstep. In the back of our minds, we felt Gillian would one day drop Nigel there, too — and then a dog? No, the logic of our position was immutable. We were parents. We knew our history. We understood our children better than they did.

Two hours later Gillian emerged from her room and asked me to join her at the dining room table again. When I faced her across the table this second time she said, "I'll give you anything you've ever wanted from me if you'll just let me have a dog. Absolutely anything."

I suddenly found myself squirming in my seat and laughing nervously to defend against her intensity.

She had made her case, had she not? I had given her a fair hearing, hadn't I? The verdict was in, right? Where was this appeal coming from? There could be no appeal. I'd already done the hard part — I'd come to a decision and given her my answer.

"I mean it, Dad, I'll do anything," she said.

I collected my senses in enough time to counter with a daring master stroke. "Would you go to La Reina?" I asked.

La Reina was the Catholic girls' school nearby. It had been a running joke and an empty threat around our house for years, whenever either of the girls got themselves into trouble that wasn't too serious for levity. "Get thee to a nunnery!" — the command of disgruntled fathers from bygone days — became: "Get thee to La Reina!"

I was so pleased with myself for thinking of this ploy. It was the perfect response to the situation. Gillian was just being a kid in promising to do *anything* for a dog; the prospect of going to La Reina, I thought, would quickly expose that promise to stark reality. But in a haunting reprise of her behavior the night I bluffed at abandoning her at the end of that dark, lonely stretch of road, she held her ground.

"For how long?" she asked.

"Ah, one year," I said, stumbling, and quickly realized I had been badly outmaneuvered. I should have said four years.

She swallowed hard; her eyes even teared up a little. "All right," she said. "For one year."

It was not my greatest moment as a decision maker. Joke or no joke, there were some very attractive aspects to Gillian's going to La Reina — even for one year. It was a good school with that Catholic knack for delivering a sound, no-nonsense education. And I was still not happy at the prospect of her returning to public school in the fall. Although our school year together had given me newfound confidence in her ability to deal with the social challenges that awaited her, I was still concerned that in classes of thirty to thirty-five students, she might fall back into some bad learning habits. I really wanted her to have a year to consolidate the gains we had made. La Reina could be just the place for that. On the other hand, I had just spent almost a solid week reaffirming my opposition to owning a dog. Was it so strong that it would prevent me from making what seemed like the best decision for Gillian's future?

I asked for another week to consider my answer.

At the end of that week Gillian signed an agreement with us obligating her to clean up her dog's messes on a daily basis, pay its food and vet bills with her own money, make an earnest effort to get into La Reina High School, and, once there, to stay there for one academic year.

I'd finally been persuaded by the depth of her commitment and the possibilities of a private school education.

On the last day of the Dan Riley School for a Girl, Gillian and I took another field trip — more modest in scope than our first, but with potentially greater ramifications for our lives. We drove sixty miles east to buy a dog. Gillian named him Marley after Bob Marley, the subject of the last film we watched together and the man who embodied her ideal of world harmony.

Appropriately enough, the first paper Gillian wrote at La Reina was about her home schooling year:

Home studies — wow, what a change that was!

I went from 7th grade, waking up each morning, taking a shower, finding something to wear, walking a mile to school, switching classes all day, stressing out about social problems and running a million miles in P.E. To 8th grade — waking up, putting on my pink panther slippers, walking down the hall and saying, "So, Dad, what are we going to learn today?"

I suddenly had no social problems. I never didn't understand what I was supposed to do; I could never slack off, and I found my father taking my best friend's place.

I was so used to the kick back atmosphere of public school. If I didn't want to be there, all I had to do was tune out and nobody would notice. I was used to writing notes when I was bored. At lunch gossiping, talking about our boyfriends' problems, and how nobody was getting along with their parents.

When I went to home studies, I found a whole new life. I have never learned so much about life and people as I did in the 8th grade. Every day I found myself in an intense conversation with my dad/teacher, talking about something that fascinated me, that I could relate to. I became a completely different person for those 9 months, living a life almost too unbelievable to last.

I did have an extremely hard time maintaining my friendships, but I did somehow manage to keep a few of them alive. Now they are all back to normal, basically, even though again this year we are going to different schools.

Home studies was an unbelievable experience, and I have very strong love/hate feelings about it. I would not do it again, but it will always stand out in my mind as one of the most memorable years of growing up.

Although she opted out after her year's commitment and is returning to public school, Gillian did not find La Reina to be the hell she had anticipated. While there, she managed to bring home the best report card we'd seen from her since early elementary school. More important, she stopped seeing most of her teachers as antagonists. She began to be open, responsive, and demonstrably appreciative of the support and encouragement she received from some of them, especially Mrs. Sears, her English teacher. One night toward the end of the year, I awoke at 1:30 A.M. to find her at the computer, literally pouring out a letter of thanks to Mrs. Sears for being so important to her during the year. Mrs. Sears's response read, in part:

Dear Jillian,

. . . Your special gifts of complex intelligence and sensitivity were evident right away in your writing. Writing truly is a window to the soul — but you knew that, right? But the wall of defenses was evident too, at first, a wall constructed very logically in order to minimize the pain resulting from dealing with the world.

You see, Dear Lady, what happened for you in the classroom wouldn't have been possible without your great courage to take a risk by letting down that wall. . . .

It was a tremendous honor to be entrusted with the extremely high quality of the risk that came from you. Moreover, it was a pleasure because of who you are and that fabulous brain of yours. As you relaxed and shared more of your logic and fascinating writing, your true talents emerged. And I had a ringside seat!

You are so special and will always have an interesting journey in life because of your unique perspectives. You will always have more insight, more asides, more humor, more capacity for pain . . . because of your giftedness — and have no doubt that you ARE gifted.

. . . Take good care of yourself. And good luck next year. . . .

It seemed that Gillian had struck the gold that the luckiest of students strike: she had met a teacher who, in time, could become a major influence on the rest of her life.

As for Marley and me? I regularly find myself cleaning up his messes — without regret or rancor. I sat with Gillian at the vet's until 1:30 the night he got stepped on by a horse. And every day I look forward to being greeted by his generous tail-wagging and our game of catch in the backyard. Through Marley, Gillian tapped into a vein of affection in me I never knew existed.

In reflecting on this discovery, I thought back to the birthday card I'd given to Meagan during the third semester of the home schooling year. At the time I was trying to respond to Meagan's growing sense of abandonment. I told her how happy I was to have two daughters, and that she should know that loving one was not the same as loving the other.

After a winter storm in New England many years ago, when she was only four, I took Meagan tobogganing at the end of our street. We took one easy glide down the hill, laughing all the way, and came to a gentle stop at the bottom. Reclining on my back, I gazed up in wonder at the white-robed trees arrayed against the new blue sky. Meagan, a little bundle of rubber boots, woolen leggings, hooded coat over knitted hat and mittens, with a cherry red cherub's face in the middle, crawled onto my stomach, put her head down on my heart, and the two of us just lay there, breathing together . . . in my mind, forever.

If my nightmare image of Meagan had been of her sending me off into the void, this was my daylight image. It didn't just come crawling out of the crevices of my imagination; it was there for me to recall in crisp detail at any waking moment. On her birthday card, I told Meagan that loving her was like breathing; like the air that day, her love is clean and sweet, filling me up and sustaining me.

But Gillian's love, I told Meagan, was a workout. She doesn't fill me up so much as she makes me sweat it out — the fats, the flab, the toxins. She makes me dig down deep inside myself to see how much love I've got and how much I'm willing to give. There's no such thing as being lazy in love with Gillian. I knew that so well after the home schooling. I'd put in so much with her — seeking to communicate, understand, and trust. It was hard, sometimes frustrating work that I would have walked away from a dozen different times except that Gillian was my flesh and blood, and you don't walk away from that.

In trying to put things in perspective for Meagan, I'd put things in perspective for myself. I realized what Gillian does for me: she keeps me fit for loving. Although she and I never went tobogganing, I have no trouble projecting her into that day I had with Meagan. With Gillian, I probably would have missed out on the wonder of the trees against the sky. I would have missed out on the bliss of father-daughter breathing. But what Gillian would have done for me would have been just as vital. She would have taken my hand, pulled me up, and led me off in search of a bigger, faster hill.